The Politics of Nothing

This book questions what sovereignty looks like when it is de-ontologised; when the nothingness at the heart of claims to sovereignty is unmasked and laid bare. Drawing on critical thinkers in political theology, such as Schmitt, Agamben, Nancy, Blanchot, Paulhan, *The Politics of Nothing* asks what happens to the political when considered in the frame of the productive potential of the nothing? The answers are framed in terms of the deep intellectual histories at our disposal for considering these fundamental questions, carving out trajectories inspired by, for example, Peter Lombard, Shakespeare and Spinoza. This book offers a series of sensitive and creative reflections that suggest the possibilities offered by thinking through sovereignty via the frame of nihilism.

This book was originally published as a special issue of *Culture, Theory and Critique.*

Clare Monagle is a lecturer in the School of Philosophical, Historical and International Studies at Monash University, Australia. She has published widely on medieval thought, and has a forthcoming monograph, *Trying Ideas: Peter Lombard, Christological Nihilism and Theological Controversy, 1050-1215.*

Dimitris Vardoulakis is a lecturer at the University of Western Sydney, Australia. He is the author of *The Doppelgänger: Literature's Philosophy* (2010) and *Sovereignty and Its Other* (forthcoming). He is also the editor of *Spinoza Now* (2011).

The Politics of Nothing

On Sovereignty

Edited by
Clare Monagle and Dimitris Vardoulakis

LONDON AND NEW YORK

First published 2013
by Routledge
2 Park Square, Milton Park, Abingdon, Oxfordshire OX14 4RN

Simultaneously published in the USA and Canada
by Routledge
711 Third Avenue, New York, NY 10017

First issued in paperback 2015

Routledge is an imprint of the Taylor & Francis Group, an informa business

British Library Cataloguing in Publication Data
A catalogue record for this book is available from the British Library

ISBN 13: 978-1-138-94661-3 (pbk)
ISBN 13: 978-0-415-50938-1 (hbk)

Typeset in Times New Roman
by Taylor and Francis Books

Publisher's Note
The publisher would like to make readers aware that the chapters in this book may be referred to as articles as they are identical to the articles published in the special issue. The publisher accepts responsibility for any inconsistencies that may have arisen in the course of preparing this volume for print.

Contents

Citation Information

The following chapters were originally published in *Culture, Theory and Critique*, volume 51, issue 2 (July 2010). When citing this material, please use the original page numbering for each article, as follows:

Chapter 2
A Sovereign Act of Negation: Schmitt's Political Theology and its Ideal Medievalism
Clare Monagle
Culture, Theory and Critique, volume 51, issue 2 (July 2010) pp. 115-127

Chapter 3
Enmity and Culture: The Rhetoric of Political Theology and the Exception in Carl Schmitt
Jürgen Fohrmann
Culture, Theory and Critique, volume 51, issue 2 (July 2010) pp. 129-144

Chapter 5
The Ends of Stasis: Spinoza as a Reader of Agamben
Dimitris Vardoulakis
Culture, Theory and Critique, volume 51, issue 2 (July 2010) pp. 145-156

Chapter 6
The Late Althusser: Materialism of the Encounter or Philosophy of Nothing?
Warren Montag
Culture, Theory and Critique, volume 51, issue 2 (July 2010) pp. 157-170

Chapter 7
Naming the Nothing: Nancy and Blanchot on Community
Ian James
Culture, Theory and Critique, volume 51, issue 2 (July 2010) pp. 171-187

Chapter 8
Next to Nothing: Jean Paulhan's Gamble
Anna-Louise Milne
Culture, Theory and Critique, volume 51, issue 2 (July 2010) pp. 189-203

Notes on Contributors

Charles Barbour lectures in Philosophy at the University of Western Sydney, Australia. Along with about a dozen book chapters, he has published on a wide variety of topics in journals such as: *Educational Philosophy and Theory*; *The Journal of Classical Sociology*; *The International Journal for Semiotics and Law*; *Law, Culture and the Humanities*; *Parallax*; *Philosophy and Social Criticism*; *Telos*; *Theory, Culture and Society*; and others. He has co-edited two collections, one on sovereignty with Routledge and one on Hannah Arendt with Continuum. He is currently working on two special issues of journals. His ongoing research projects concern questions of mendacity, on the one hand, and equality, on the other. His monograph, *The Marx Machine: Politics, Polemics, Ideology*, is available from Lexington.

Jürgen Fohrmann is Rector at the University of Bonn, Germany. His several books include *Projekt der deutschen Literaturgeschichte. Entstehung und Scheitern einer nationalen Poesiegeschichtsschreibung zwischen Humanismus und Deutschem Kaiserreich* (1989) and, as editor or co-editor, *Politische Theologie. Formen und Funktionen im 20. Jahrhundert* (2003) and *1848 und das Versprechen der Moderne* (2003).

Ian James completed his doctoral research on the fictional and theoretical writings of Pierre Klossowski at the University of Warwick in 1996. Since then he has been a Fellow and Lecturer in French at Downing College, University of Cambridge, UK. He is the author of *Pierre Klossowski: The Persistence of a Name* (Legenda, 2000), *The Fragmentary Demand: An Introduction to the Philosophy of Jean-Luc Nancy* (Stanford University Press, 2006), and *Paul Virilio* (Routledge, 2007).

Anna-Louise Milne is a senior lecturer in the Department of French and Comparative Studies at the University of London Institute in Paris, France. Notable publications are two books on Jean Paulhan (*The Extreme In-Between. Jean Paulhan's Place in the Twentieth Century*, Legenda 2006, and *La Correspondance Paulhan-Belaval*, Gallimard, 2005), and a recent contribution to the current centenary of the *Nouvelle Revue Française* in the form of a special issue of the *Romanic Review* on the relations between Gallimard's foundational review and modernism. Her current research spins out of the centre/periphery dynamic explored in construction of the literary field, to consider its modalities in twentieth-century visions of and for the city of Paris.

Clare Monagle is a lecturer in the School of Philosophical, Historical and International Studies at Monash University, Australia. Her speciality is the intellectual history of

Medieval Europe. She received her PhD from the Johns Hopkins University in 2007. She has published articles in *Viator, Parergon* and *Postmedieval*. Her forthcoming monograph on Peter Lombard is under contract with Brepols.

Warren Montag is Professor of English and Comparative Literature at Occidental College in Los Angeles, USA. His books include *Louis Althusser* (2002) and *Bodies, Masses, Power: Spinoza and his Contemporaries* (1999), as well as the edited volume *The New Spinoza* (1997), with Ted Stolze.

Dimitris Vardoulakis is a lecturer at the University of Western Sydney, Australia. His publications include *The Doppelgänger: Literature's Philosophy* (Fordham University Press, 2010). Other edited or co-edited volumes include *Spinoza Now* (Universtiy of Minnesota Press, 2010), *The Political Animal* (in *Substance* journal, 2008), *After Blanchot* (Delaware University Press, 2005), and *The Politics of Place* (in *Angelaki* journal, 2004).

Introduction: The Negativity of Sovereignty, Now

Clare Monagle and Dimitris Vardoulakis

The title of this collection is inspired by Georges Bataille's famous formulation: 'Sovereignty is NOTHING' (1980: 300). Here, Bataille suggested that sovereignty resides in the ecstatic moment of forgetting, outside of knowledge, chronology and causality. For Bataille, sovereignty exists only in moments of absence, only when referentiality is abandoned and the nothing is paramount. It can only be known on the *via negativa*, through its effects of, for example, horror, disgust, hysteria, elation or intoxication. Bataille's gesture was to move the concept of sovereignty beyond the juridical, towards subjectivity in the broadest sense. The subject experiences sovereignty through the miraculous moment of rupture into the nothing, which, in turn, itself ruptures the coherence of the subject.

Bataille's statement may appear too obscure or 'metaphysical' in a world that became obsessed with questions about sovereignty after the events on September 11, 2001. Much of the legal debate that took place in the United States, for example, about the correct treatment of enemy combatants hinged on whether or not suspected terrorists should be understood to be citizens of sovereign states, and therefore permitted the protections of the Geneva Convention. And many critical readings of the presidency of George W. Bush were concerned by his extra-judicial decisions, concerned at the presidential assertion of his own exceptional sovereign powers at the expense of due process. The *realpolitik* of sovereignty, expressed through questions about who has it and what it really means, has been laid bare in the international politics of the post-9/11 world.

It is this political context that makes Bataille's gnomic statement that 'Sovereignty is NOTHING' indispensable for beginning a conversation about sovereignty and modernity. In spite of the seeming opaqueness of Bataille's words, his assertion speaks to both modernist and post-modernist unmaskings of the nothing at the core of sovereignty. That is, much twentieth-century theoretical writing has been concerned to show how sovereign claims to authority are always grasping towards an illusory universality. They claim an always deferred higher power as a source of legitimacy. Bataille's proclamation of the nothing at the heart of sovereignty is emblematic of these larger inquiries into the assumptions that generate legitimacy in culture and politics. As such, it functions as a hermeneutic informing this collection of essays. They each seek to consider what happens to sovereignty when its profound nothingness is made explicit. What does this do to conceptualisations of sovereignty? How can a politics be articulated in the face of the nothing?

According to Oliver Roy, one response to the modern understanding of the impossibility of sovereignty can be seen in the actions of Islamic fundamentalists whose actions emanate from the desire to attain pure religion.[1] That is, they resist the idea of a governmental structure that would claim to mediate sovereignty from a higher authority to a general population. Rather, they are driven by a fantasy of the creation of a pan-Islamic community that would transcend the sovereign state, in favour of deculturation in the service of salvation. This manifests as a war on culture, as that which stands between the individual and his God. This is a politics that refuses the distinction of the political as a category, fusing public and private, heaven and earth, and human and divine temporalities. Islamic fundamentalists actively refuse the aspiration of the creation of sovereign entities, preferring instead to proffer an eschatological politics that is always just about to deliver transcendence and bounty. On the other hand, the US and their allies have replied to the terrorist threat through imperialist gestures such as the invasion of Afghanistan and Iraq. Where al Qaeda have refused the idea of sovereignty, conventionally understood, the US and the Coalition of the willing have sought to bolster their own sovereignty through the exercise of force and the use of exceptional powers within their respective domestic situations.

International politics post-9/11 has exposed this fault line, between nation states intent on maintaining their sovereign authority over territories and populations, and terrorist groups desiring to combust the sovereignties of modernity in favour of eschatology. This has been particularly clear in the language used by neo-conservatives to characterise al Qaeda. For Rumsfeld, Wolfowitz, and others, Bin Laden and his followers represent a dangerous medieval force. The argument went that due to their lack of interest in conventional sovereignty, and their lack of respect for the rule of law, al Qaeda placed themselves outside of modernity's telos. Hence, partly, from this line of argument came the justification for the use of torture on the part of the neocons. As has already been mentioned, as non-moderns, who refuse identification with the sovereign state, it was argued in the 'Torture Memos' that alleged terrorists need not be afforded the general protections laid out in the Geneva Convention.

In so many ways, then, sovereignty has erupted as an urgent issue in a variety of fields – philosophy, political science, legal theory, international relations and so on. However, as Jens Bartelsen has recently showed, the debate in all these fields is marred by a trenchant opposition between two sides. For one group of scholars, the challenges posed by the post-9/11 landscape affords an appreciation of how the forces of globalisation have diminished the power of state sovereignty, arguing that 'crucial features of state sovereignty have been weakened, such as its ability to make and enforce laws, the power to define and defend territorial borders, as well as the capacity to shape and direct economic performance' (2006: 466). Other scholars, on the other hand, maintain the efficacy and necessity of sovereignty as a concept underpinning political life, and argue that what is going on at present is a resetting of the relationship between constituting and constituted power. Sovereignty, here, is reified as the inevitable manifestation of political life. In the former frame, sovereignty is under threat as a result of global capital and market economies. For the former, sovereignty may change its operations, but will essentially remain a concept that underpins governmentality and the state. In order to disentangle this antinomy, Bartelson (2006) insightfully observes that neither side is aware enough of the ontological status of the concept of sovereignty. Wendy Brown (2008) implicitly shares this view in arguing that sovereignty retains as its central core the fiction of the autonomy of the political – a fiction whose ontological status is theological. Our inability to unpack that fiction leaves us in sovereignty's thrall, and 'prevents political thought that is in its grip from reckoning with the nature of sovereignty's practical breakdown and re-located trace effects, and above all from reckoning with capital's historically unprecedented powers of domination' (2008: 252).

Bataille's statement that 'Sovereignty is NOTHING' speaks to Bartelson and Brown's insights. In its apophatic energy, it reads sovereignty's implicit theology as a nothing. Sovereignty is never given, as Bodin famously put it, because of its ontological status – its being theological, and hence unfounded on any social practice or discursive justification.[2] In other words, its ontological status is nothing. Sovereignty *is* nothing, inasmuch as we refuse its always present, if somewhat latent, theological claims. The implications of this recognition for thought and practice are vast, but there are three primary concerns in relation to the understanding of the political in modernity, and which concern us in this volume.

The first concern relates to whether negativity divests discourse of any serious political weight. This is the spectre of the 'dialectic of nihilism', as Gillian Rose (1984) called it. The fear named by Rose is that understanding the nothing of sovereignty would result in paralysis of praxis. The most common line of argument asserts that the nothing or negativity inscribed in the structures of power that many 'post-structuralists adumbrate ultimately leads to vacuous formulations, mere word-play. The notion of sovereignty's negativity undermines the capacity for intellectual or political foundations, within the nothing, there can be no basis for action and a descent into anomie. As a consequence, the nothing is here understood as being divorced from politics, as being unable to have any impact in the way institutions are formed or the law is exercised. This combative attitude harks back to the first modern text that used the term 'nihilism', Jacobi's open letter to Fichte (Jacobi: 1994).[3] In this letter, Jacobi chastised the adherents for transcendental realism for their tendency, as he had it, to be less interested in the reality of the material world than in the subjective experiences that produce knowledge. For Jacobi, this philosophy was unmoored from the real, and therefore resulted in a pointless nihilism.

The inevitability of nihilism when sovereignty is recognised as nothing is an idea refuted by Anna-Louise Milne in her chapter for this volume, 'Next to Nothing: Jean Paulhan's Gamble'. Drawing on Paulhan's *Les Fleurs de Tarbes*, she argues that the author distinguishes between the nothingness that he held to characterise the Nazi occupation, and the 'small nothings' of custom and habitus that sustain life. In so doing, she refutes claims that Paulhan's work was apolitical, challenging readings that consider Paulhan's thought to be aporetic. Charles Barbour's chapter 'The Sovereign without Domain: George Bataille and the Ethics of Nothing' refutes the tendency of some scholars to impute a mystical nihilism on the part of Bataille, without recognising the fundamentally ethical dimensions of Bataille's embrace of the nothing. That is, Barbour argues, Bataille's assertion of sovereignty's nothingness is in part a repudiation of the servility and waste endemic to sovereignty in its mainstream meanings. Bataille is also a central figure in Ian James' 'Naming and Nothing: Nancy and Blanchot on Community'. In this chapter, James considers the exchanges between Nancy and Blanchot on the nature of community. James shows that both thinkers, in spite of many disagreements, shared the project of thinking community in the light of the absence of transcendent principles that could guarantee authority. James shows how they negotiate their conversation, partly, through their readings of Bataille's affirmation that 'Sovereignty is NOTHING'.

3

The second concern canvassed in this volume is the opposite of the first, in that it insists of the political significance of the nothing or negativity. As Carl Schmitt argues, sovereignty 'looked at normatively ... emanates from nothingness' (Schmitt 1985: 31-32). This line of argument goes back at least to Hegel.[4] It is often concerned with the way the sacred figures within the secular, with how the theological trace manifests or lingers or erupts in political discourses that claim to be worldly. Most post-World War II political theory can be read from this perspective, from Althusser's post-Marxism to the famous debate between Nancy (1991) and Blanchot (1988) about Bataille, and from Ernesto Laclau's concept of the 'empty signifier' (1996) to Giorgio Agamben's more recent argument that the notion of the exception is based on an analogy between justice and negative theology (1998). The common denominator of this approach is that nothingness is here regarded in positive terms. The debate now is about to realise the productive potential of the nothing, of negativity. In this theoretical frame, the nothing opens up a vista of opportunity to rethink political and ethical verities. The nothing, here, forces a reconsideration of the very basis of political commitments, one that takes the refusal of ontology as its generative starting point.

This is not to say that starting something from nothing is easy. A number of chapters in this collection respond to these attempts to think through the nothing, and show the intractability of doing so. For example, in 'A Sovereign Act of Negation: Schmitt's Political Theology and its Ideal Medievalism' Clare Monagle excavates Carl Schmitt's fantasy about the Middle Ages, upon which his political theology is premised. When faced with sovereignty's nothingness, she argues, Schmitt takes recourse in a historical vision that privileges the Medieval Church as a long-lost site of unity and pure politics, himself inscribing a historical ontology of sorts. Jürgen Fohrmann's 'The Rhetoric on Political Theology and the Exception in Carl Schmitt' offers another reflection on the foundations of Carl Schmitt's notion of the exception. Fohrmann draws on a comparison between Schmitt and Benjamin's readings of *Hamlet*, in order to explore Schmitt's reluctance to depart from a figure of foundation. The exception, even when Schmitt secularises the concept, necessitates an instant of transcending that is eschatological.

In 'The Late Althusser: Materialism of the Encounter or Philosophy of Nothing?', Warren Montag argues that in one of his later works, Althusser deploys the Lucretian notion of the 'void' as a way to understand both unfolding chronology, as well as the singularity of the momentary, producing as Montag says 'a theory of messianicity without a messiah'. Here, the nothing, paradoxically, enables a return to the sacred. A sacred, however, divested of the divine. In 'The Ends of Stasis: Spinoza as a Reader of Agamben', Dimitris Vardoulakis shows how the diseased bare life of the *Musulmann* functions for Agamben as a zone of indistinction, separable from politics. This bare life, Vardoulakis argues, is both the nothing and the end in Agamben's thought. Agamben thus founds a theory of sovereignty, and concomitantly on ethics, upon the passivity of bare life which he reads, following Spinoza, as a site of absolute immanence. Vardoulakis explores how this theory of the nothing of sovereignty turns on itself, and projects a totalising discourse with its own sovereign claims.

The third aspect considered within this collection is, in fact, a symptom of the previous two, and permeates all of the chapters in this collection to some degree. It is the recognition that politics in modernity is inescapably linked to the way nothingness is related to sovereignty. This is an understanding of temporality, that sees sovereignty's nothingness as not merely a symptom of modernity, but in fact one of its defining features. In this telling, modernity is haunted by its absent ontology, in a double bind

4

of presence and absence. And because of its centrality to the condition of modernity, the nothing of sovereignty is not a problem that remains confined within political theory. Rather, it permeates every practice that aspires to modernity, in any form. The aforementioned, Jean Paulhan (2006), for example, offered an instance of this when we recognise how sign-posted his study of literature with the notion of the nothing. It is also implicit in Derrida's repeated assertion that deconstruction is a challenge to all forms of sovereignty.[5] The poetics offered by the photographic negative also comes into play here, as the power of negation that structures modern forms of vision, and representation (see Cadava 1997 and Agacinski 2003). It may not be an overstatement to say that nothing is modernity's trace.

In the context of sovereignty, however, modernity should not be understood as a temporal signifier separated from the past. Rather, as the theological provenance of sovereignty's negativity indicates, sovereignty retains its past as remnants that it refuses to shed. Moreover, as Vardoulakis has recently argued in *Sovereignty and its Other* (2013), such remnants are instrumental in the strategies of the justification of violence employed by sovereignty. So, modernity here does not signify a static temporal category, but rather the moment of the *now* as it is related in various modalities and articulations, connections and disjunction, to past expression of sovereignty.

Notes

1 Roy's position is developed over two books (1994 and 2004). From this perspective, Carl Schmitt's (2007) description of the partisan is the complete opposite of today's al Qaeda and other fundamentalists – including Christian Evangelists – since the partisan always includes in his aim the creation of a sovereign state.

2 '[T]he people or the aristocracy of a commonwealth can purely and simply give someone absolute and perpetual power to dispose of all possession, person, and the entire state at his pleasure, and then to leave it to anyone he pleases, just a proprietor can make a pure and simple gift of his goods for no other reason than his generosity. This is a true gift because it carries no further conditions, being complete and accomplished all at once, whereas gifts that carry obligations and conditions are not authentic gifts. And so sovereignty given to a prince subject to obligations and conditions is properly not sovereignty or absolute power' (Bodin 1992: 7-8).

3 For a discussion of this letter, see Vardoulakis (2010, chapter 1).

4 See, for example, the fascinating exchange of letters between Carl Schmitt and Alexandre Kojève about Hegel (1998).

5 For Derrida's most important discussion on sovereignty see Derrida (2005).

References

Agacinski, S. 2003. *Time Passing: Modernity and Nostalgia.* Translated by J. Gladding. New York: Columbia University Press.

Agamben, G. 1998. *Homo Sacer: Sovereign Power and Bare Life.* Translated by D. Heller-Roazen. Stanford: Stanford University Press.

Bartelson, J. 2006. 'The Concept of Sovereignty Revisited'. *European Journal of International Law* 17.2, 463–74.

Bataille, G. 1980. *OEuvres complètes,* volume 8. Paris, Gallimard.

Blanchot, M. 1988. *The Unavowable Community.* Translated by P. Joris. Barrytown, NY: Station Hill Press.

Bodin, J. 1992. *On Sovereignty: Four Chapters from the Six Books of the Commonwealth.* Edited and translated by Julian H. Franklin. Cambridge: Cambridge University Press.

Brown, W. 2008. 'Sovereignty and the Return of the Repressed'. In D. Campbell and M. Schoolman (eds), *The New Pluralism: William Connolly and the Contemporary Global Condition* (pp. 250–273). Durham, NC: Duke University Press,.

Cadava, E. 1997. *Words of Light: Theses on the Photography of History.* Princeton, NJ: Princeton University Press.

Derrida, J. 2005. *Rogues: Two Essays on Reason.* Translated by P.-A. Brault & M. Nass. Stanford, CA: Stanford University Press.

Jacobi, F. H. 1994. 'Jacobi to Fichte'. In *The Main Philosophical Writings and the Novel 'Allwill'.* Translated by G. di Giovanni. Montreal & Kingston: McGill-Queen's University Press.

Laclau, E. 1996. *Emancipation(s).* London: Verso.

Nancy, J.-L. 1991. *The Inoperative Community.* Translated by P. Connor et al. Minneapolis, MN: University of Minnesota Press.

Paulhan, J. 2006. *The Flowers of Tarbes, or, Terror in Literature.* Translated by M. Syrotinski. Urbana, IL: University of Illinois Press.

Rose, G. 1984. Dialectic of Nihilism: Post-Structuralism and Law. Oxford: Blackwell.

Roy, O. 1994. *The Failure of Political Islam.* Translated by C. Volk. Cambridge, MA: Harvard University Press.

Roy, O. 2004. *Globalized Islam: The Search for a New Ummah.* New York: Columbia University Press.

Schmitt, C. 1985. *Political Theology: Four Chapters on the Concept of Sovereignty.* Translated by G. D. Schwab. Cambridge, MA: MIT Press.

Schmitt, C. 2007. *Theory of the Partisan.* Translated by G. L. Ulmen. New York: Telos Press.

Schmitt, C. and Kojève, A. 1998. 'Der Briefwechsel Kojève – Schmitt'. Edited by P. Tomissen. *Schmittiana* 6, 100–24.

Vardoulakis, D. 2010. *The Doppelgänger: Literature's Philosophy.* New York: Fordham University Press.

Vardoulakis, D. 2013. *Sovereignty and Its Other: Toward the Dejustification of Violence.* New York: Fordham University Press.

A Sovereign Act of Negation: Schmitt's Political Theology and its Ideal Medievalism

Clare Monagle

Abstract *This article argues that Carl Schmitt's political theology is premised on an idealised and totalising vision of the Middle Ages. That is, he casts modern political concepts as debased and corrupt in comparison to the proper politics of the Medieval Church, as he sees it. Drawing on a historically contextualised reading of the Fourth Lateran Council, which took place in 1215, the article's author argues that Schmitt's medieval comparison is much more complicated than he suggests. Schmitt's historical vision is, thus, a wilful projection of unity onto a diverse and distant past.*

Carl Schmitt's model of political theology is premised upon an idealised Roman Catholic Middle Ages in which there is no separation between the political and the sacred. His indictment of the delusions and corruptions of political concepts in modernity is premised on his perfected point of origin, that of *unum sanctum*, one holy catholic apostolic church. This paper seeks to question Schmitt's medieval foundation in two ways. First, I will extricate Schmitt's Middle Ages through a reading of his notion of the Modern. Second, I will contrast his vision of medieval politics with an example of a statement of sovereignty that is actually medieval. This example of the Constitutions of the Lateran Council of 1215 will demonstrate that the medievalised political vision of Schmitt is a totalising projection, rather than a demonstrably reliable vision of the past.[1]

The Fourth Lateran Council of 1215 looks, on the one hand, like Schmitt's medieval moment *par excellence*. Its pronouncements constitute one of the most decisive statements of papal sovereignty of the Middle Ages. It is

---

[1] David Nirenberg, of Johns Hopkins University and the University of Chicago, provided my first experience of Carl Schmitt in his graduate seminar at Hopkins. I dedicate this article to him. Gaby Spiegel also from the Johns Hopkins Univerisity, read this in her customary generous and scouring manner, and made some very help-ful suggestions. In addition, I would like to thank the School of Historical Studies at Monash University for listening to, and commenting upon, this paper. In particular, Jane Drakard, Constant Mews, Michael Hau and Barbara Caine provided useful comments in a gentle environment. And of course, many thanks to Dimitris Vardoulakis for his always sage advice.

concerned with precisely the properly political agenda that Schmitt sees as foundational in medieval Europe, that of the clear articulation of amities and enmities authorised by the proximity of the papacy to the sacred. This Council defines the boundaries of Christendom, via the demarcation of its borders both in a theological and spatial sense. The papacy defines Christendom as a sovereign political unit in its clear opposition to its enemies: heretics within and infidels outside.

On the other hand, the recourse to the sacred as an authorising and boundary-setting force is far more contingent and qualified than Schmitt would suggest. The Constitutions of Lateran IV actually articulate a paradoxically anti-theological epistemology. That is, in order to justify its assertion of sovereignty, the papacy produces a model of human access to truth and divinity that is fragmented and timorous. Rather than the Schmittian vision of bold political formulations produced in the authority of *unum sanctum*, we see a displacement of the political from the sacred into the always marginal operations of human language. The Council performs this shift through its endorsement of the systematic theology of Peter Lombard, who stands in more broadly in this context for the proto-scholastic curriculum of the schools of Paris. At the time when the Papacy is making one of its strongest statements of centralised, sovereign authority, it is also enshrining an approach to doctrine which is dialectical, rational and notional in its orientation. This medieval moment of sovereignty is brokered analytically via a move away from a notion of language as infused with divinity, towards a notion of language as always compromised in its capacity to represent Divine Truth. The complicated political theology of Lateran IV suggests that the politically sublime Catholic formulation of Schmitt, which he casts in such glowing relation to the Modern, is a problematic simplification.

According to Schmitt, famously, the sovereign is the one 'who decides on the exception' (Schmitt 1985: 5). And, 'The state of exception in jurisprudence is analogous to the miracle in theology' (Schmitt 1985: 36). This analogy supposes the correspondence between the exception and the miracle and between jurisprudence and theology. One implication of this distinction is an assertion of the gulf between the medieval and the modern. The medieval is Catholic and its hypostatic moment, when immanence and transcendence are co-joined, is the miracle. The modern, however, is governed by jurisprudence, the ostensibly rational body of law that constitutes the legal life of the state. According to Schmitt's logic, the real moment of actualisation of the claims to authority of that jurisprudence is the state of exception when the sovereign suspends those laws on the authority vested in him from somewhere else, often indeterminate. The reason for this indeterminacy is, according to Schmitt, that 'all significant concepts of the modern theory of the state are secularised theological concepts' (Schmitt 1985: 36). The modern, therefore, denies its medieval self. Modern theories of the state cloak their claims to Presence in rationalist discourse.

The effect of this formulation is to posit the necessity of a trace of Presence in modern theories of the state, which can be deployed by the sovereign as the site of his authority to render the exception. That is, the sovereign needs recourse to a transcendental claim in order to justify the status of exception. The corollary is – in terms of the analogy between the exception and the miracle – that medieval theories of the state were likewise informed by a confidence in Presence, communicated by the miracle. The difference is, however, that this notion of Presence was the explicit foundation of statements of sovereignty, rather than something veiled and surreptitious. This is because where the modern state has jurisprudence, the medieval has theology at its core. The positive statement of God's existence, that is the basis of theology, is the point of origin for confidence in the Holy Roman Catholic church and her institutions.

Is Schmitt right in this reading of the medieval? And, does it matter if he is not? What is the implication, logically, if the analogy between the exception and miracle, between jurisprudence and theology, does not hold up? The consequence would be the refusal of Schmitt's implicitly historical formulation. His point was that modern theories of the state mask a vestigially medieval orientation towards the hypostasis of the exception. Schmitt's historical explanation for this trace was that the past four hundred years of European history need to be understood as a reaction to the theological and political turmoil of the sixteenth century, whereby the unity of Christendom had been repressed and reformed into petty nation-states.[2] The violent conflict of the reformation and counter-reformation necessitated the development of a theologically neutralised political language, one that would enable agreement and compromise in an increasingly fractured Europe. But this move could not evacuate theological concepts, they were merely deferred into secularised and 'depoliticised' linguistic formulations over the course of the following four hundred years. By 'depoliticised' Schmitt meant that political language moved away, after the Reformation, from clearly articulating the friend/enemy distinction that he held to be crucial to the operation of the political. He wrote that 'all political concepts, images and terms have a polemical meaning. They are focused on a specific conflict and are bound to a concrete-situation; the result (which manifests itself in war or revolution) is a friend-enemy grouping' (Schmitt 1976: 30). The logical inference of Schmitt's historical line is that, in the pre-modern period when Europe was united as Christendom, the certainty manifest by a theologically authorised polity meant that the friend/enemy distinction could be made without ambivalence or qualification. The combination of Schmitt's analogue between miracle and exception and his idea of a post-reformation 'depoliticization', posits a medieval foundation for the political as he understands it. The political, under this rubric, constitutes the possibility of definitive statements as to the nature of the friend/enemy distinction that produces polities and the language that makes them.

In *Roman Catholicism and Political Form*, Schmitt's identification with pre-modern Catholic Europe as an ideal political unit is explicit (Schmitt 1996). He espouses, according to John McCormick, a 'clerico-conservative vision of Europe' which would reject the sacralisation of privacy that he holds to characterise economic and social liberalism (McCormick 1998). The embrace of privacy takes enmity and friendship out of the public sphere and so divests

---

[2] See Schmitt (1993). For one pertinent discussion of this work, see Thompson (2005).

public life of its political momentum. We see again here Schmitt's notion of the historical movement towards the neutralisation of politics within modernity. Modernity's focus on privacy and interiority renders decisions about enmity as personal and subjective, rather than procedural and objective. Schmitt argues that a properly Catholic Europe, on the other hand, would refuse this evasion wrought by privacy and insist upon a substantively political orientation. This orientation would be necessary as the interests of the individual would be merged with that of the Church. The goal of spiritual salvation would be entirely interwoven with the success of the political institution of the Church. Within this structure, there is no need for privacy as the highest expression of interiority would be in the service of the transcendental ideal of *Ecclesia*. For Schmitt, in *Roman Catholicism and Political Form*, the Catholic Church is the historical institution that has most successfully manifested its politics without a disingenuous denial of its profoundly political orientation. The Catholic Church, as a hypothetical polity, would see no contradiction between the divisive articulation of its friends and enemies and the drive towards ontological purity.

It does matter then, whether or not Schmitt is right in his articulation of the Catholic Middle Ages. His two seminal distinctions about the exception and about the friend/enemy, both depend upon an ideal of pre-modernity that actualises a genuine politics that the modern cannot access due to the accretion of depoliticised and neutralised language. Without the medieval foundation, he would not have the theology that haunts modernity. His lament for what has been lost is dependent upon his conservative historical vision of the Middle Ages, which is constituted by a clerical hegemony informed by faith.

Schmitt's critique of liberalism has had tremendous influence across the political spectrum. This is well-known and need not be rehearsed in detail here.[3] In particular, Schmitt has been deployed by theorists keen to interrogate and problematise the notions of neutrality and universalism inhering within the political languages of liberalism. As Chantal Mouffe points out, the ideas of Carl Schmitt 'allow us to acknowledge – and, therefore, be in a better position to try to negotiate – an important paradox inscribed in the very nature of liberal democracy' (Mouffe 2000: 37). Schmitt's critique of liberalism, grounded in the historical genealogy I have set up above, has challenged a number of its fundamental tenets. This has forced, particularly in the work of Mouffe and Giorgio Agamben, a serious and productive engagement with the ideas of Carl Schmitt. While remaining highly critical of Schmitt's most absolutising claims, scholars have engaged his provocative distinctions as a means to better understand contemporary political communities, desires and apparatus. Mouffe again, 'Schmitt is an adversary from whom we can learn, because we can draw on his insights. Turning them against him, we should use them to formulate a better understanding of liberal democracy, one that acknowledges its paradoxical nature' (Mouffe 2000: 57).

---

[3] Most famously, see Agamben (1998). See also Agamben (2005). Chantal Mouffe has also made significant use of Schmitt, see Mouffe (1999; 2000).

Schmitt's insights as to the nature of medieval political life, as the site of a foundational genuine politics grounded in an absolute distinction between friend and enemy, is one that can be 'turned against him'. This is why I want in this article to challenge his vision of the past by recourse to a more nuanced historical analysis. If we can assess Schmitt's vision of the past against a more involved historical panorama, it will enable a small insight into the limits of his thought, a vista upon the fantasies and its projections that inform his vision of political life. Schmitt's articulation of the Catholic Middle Ages, when challenged, is a way into further understanding both the power and the limitations of his prophetically-tinged political visions.

What then of the medieval? What did a medieval political elaboration look like? Hence, we turn now to the aforementioned example of Lateran IV in 1215. Does this example yield a properly politicised and non-neutral set of terms? Can the medieval be made to do the work that Schmitt would have it do as foil to the modern?

It cannot. Lateran IV proffers its own strategy of neutralisation, in that it attempts to carve out a sphere of appropriate and ratified political language that is deemed to function without the apprehension of direct Divine Presence. Yes, at this Council the Church does rely on the petrine dispensation as a source for its own authority. It does claim Divine Origin. But it does not claim that this dispensation unfolds progressively in the work of history. It is not an accessible agent of truth. Instead, in the constitutions of that Council it was stated that 'between the Creator and a creature there can be remarked no similarity so great that a greater dissimilarity cannot be seen between them'.[4] First and foremost, the Council was determined to point out the fundamental inadequacy of human knowledge of the divine. But, at this same Council, a crusade was preached, the doctrine of transubstantiation was officially put on the books, all heretics were condemned, and Peter Lombard's theology was endorsed. This was a watershed Council for the medieval church, and its documents constituted one of the strongest statements of papal primacy of the pre-modern era.[5] Sandwiched within these expressions of papal theory and intent, however, was the statement of negative theology written above. As it went about defining and consolidating definitions of Christendom, this same Council declared that the principle of dissimilarity should always underlie any rendering of God's being by man. That principle is that what can be construed as human positive knowledge can – at best – work to indicate what God is not. The overall function of the Council – as discernable from its constitutions – was the construction of a fortified, united Christendom. Among the positive assertions of sovereign power, however, was this reminder of the fragility of human knowledge and man's ultimate distance from his Maker.

Institution building and negative theology might seem to be incongruous partners. As Derrida has it, 'negative theology consists of considering that

---

[4] Alberigo (1972): 'quia inter creatorem et creaturam non potest tanta similitudo notari, quin inter eos maior sit dissimilitudo notanda'. Translated in Rothwell (1975: 645).

[5] On Lateran IV, see Mews and Monagle (2010). See also Robb (1997) and Marion (2002).

every predicative language is inadequate to the essence, in truth to the hyperessentiality (the being beyond Being) of God; consequently only a negative ("apophatic") attribution can claim to approach God, and to prepare us for a silent intuition of God' (Derrida 1989: 4). In the terms of medieval Christianity, negative theology constitutes the refusal of the possibility that the ontic logos might bear Presence into the terms of human language.[6] Instead, God must be apprehended on the *via negativa*. He is to be found interstitially in the assertions that language makes about things, concepts. He is found there, because he is none of those things and can be recognised by his absence. To paraphrase Derrida, God is written completely otherwise, He cannot be in these terms (Derrida 1989: 4). Therefore it is only known what he is not. The statement of Lateran IV that 'between the Creator and a creature there can be remarked no similarity so great that a greater dissimilarity cannot be seen between them' (Alberigo 1972: 232) reflects that same refusal of predicability as described by Derrida, the appearance of similarity between man and God can only be understood as a semiotic bridge to greater knowledge of the distance between them.

How then does the statement of negative theology at Lateran IV, and its limitation of the possibility of the predication of positive attributes of God, cohere with the assertion of papal primacy and direction of papal action of that Council? For negative theology appears to be anti-foundational, in that it derogates the productive capacities of language to produce a positive system of representation which might legitimate action. But the overall mood evinced from the records of the Council was not simply one of timidity in the light of God's inscrutability. Rather, the Council proceeded – on the whole – with a degree of confidence. Drawing on the warrant of 'the keys of the church, which Jesus Christ Himself granted to the apostles and their successors',[7] the Constitutions of Lateran IV proudly asserted the mandate granted to the papacy by the petrine dispensation of Matthew 16:18, 'you are Peter, and on this rock I will build my Church'. In its confident assertion of apostolic succession, Innocent III's papacy declared itself authorised to continue that dispensation. *Ecclesia* lived and breathed, in the ongoing nature of revelation. Its task was continual vigilance to keep the world safe for sacraments, so that the duty of mediating salvation could be performed. Consequently, 'between the Creator and a creature there can be remarked no similarity so great that a greater dissimilarity cannot be seen between them'. The gap between God and Man was profound, with the exception of the infusion of grace achieved sacramentally, through the intervention of a priest. The important word of this formulation is 'remarked' [*notari*]. It is not possible to denote, to describe, or to inscribe the similarity between God and Man. But, as the constitutions of the Council remind, *ecclesia* can solve that separation through the mini-hypostases of the sacraments.

The sacraments, then, are the only conduit to a direct experience of God. Any other apprehension of Presence must proceed with the knowledge of the

---

[6] An excellent introduction to negative theology can be found in Milem (2007).

[7] Alberigo (1972: 232): 'claves ecclesiae, quas ipse concessit apostolis et eorum successoribus Iesus Christus'. Translated in Rothwell (1975: 644).

chasm of dissimilarity that precludes an immediate relationship. Lateran IV thus declares the monopoly of the papacy over direct access to the Divine. If the direct experience of Grace can only be achieved through the mystical nature of the sacraments, then it is clearly owned by *Ecclesia*. To think about God notionally or metaphorically, then, is inherently limited and contingent. Jean-Luc Marion writes that negative theology is used 'to place God at a great distance from the concept of metaphysics' (Marion 2002: 129). This is precisely the point of the formulation of Lateran IV: the irreducibility between God and man frees human language from the compulsion to imagine the hyper-essentiality of God. Writing, inscription or remarking are better, therefore, put to the use of edification and discipline in the creaturely world, as the constitutions of Lateran IV imply. Marion says that this use of negative theology constitutes a 'pragmatic theology of absence' (Marion 2002: 155). It is pragmatic because it eschews the possibility that mystical revelation might be the basis for a positive, linguistic knowledge of the essence of the Divine. Instead, it suggests that the dissimilarity between God and man might be a foundation for a linguistic theology that embraces the contingencies of language as productive. In this case, the strategic deployment of negative theology in the constitutions of Lateran IV makes the case that even the predication of being upon God is to presume an impossible and essential knowledge of Him. Language, of course, can and will be used to predicate things of God. The important point being, as the constitutions of Lateran IV reminded, that this predication be affirmed as contingent, arbitrary and notional. This frees human language from the failure of not registering God properly. Instead, it is a notion that affirms the semiotic possibilities of language within the relativised world of multiplicity. This is the sovereign act of negation of the Papacy, it is to confirm that since human statements of the nature of God's being must bear the assumption of fundamental dissimilarity to God himself, one can therefore presume language to build knowledge in the world without imperilling sacred truth.

This distinction made between mystical and cognitive knowledge of God in the constitutions of Lateran IV has a complicated context in the politics of pedagogy in the twelfth and thirteenth centuries. This statement of negative theology occurred in the course of a defence of the Christology of Peter Lombard, who had been one of the premier theologians of the twelfth century. Lombard had been accused of Christological Nihilism in his *Sententiae*,[8] of minimising Christ's humanity in his explanation of the hypostasis. That is, in his efforts to explain just how Christ could constitute God and Man in the same instance, he had been charged with a heterodox linguistic formulation of the relationship between them. Of course, debates about the efficacy of the new linguistic theology emerging in the schools – as opposed to the mystically oriented theology of the monasteries – were nothing new. Before Peter Lombard, Berengar of Tours, Abelard and Gilbert of Poitiers, had each felt the wrath of those who considered their investigation

---

[8] The standard edition of the *Sententiae* is Peter Lombard (1971–1981). On Lombard see Colish (1994). This work remains the most extensive and authoritative treatment of Lombard's life and career in any language. The best general introduction is Rosemann (2004).

into the nature of sacred words to be contradictory to the simplicity of belief demanded of the faithful.[9] Simply, each of these theologians had applied the practice of dialectic to sacred doctrines, such as the Eucharist or the Trinity. And consequently, each had felt the ire of more mystically-oriented critics who preferred to approach theological concerns through the rubric of prayer and meditation, rather than through the application of dialectical reasoning. As a result of these conflicts, all three of Berengar, Abelard and Gilbert of Poitiers had been subject to papal censure.

The *Sententiae* of Peter Lombard, in particular, attracted the ire of critics. The reason for this ire was that the *Sententiae* was not just a work of exposition but, unlike his predecessors, proposed new a new theological synthesis. Also, unlike the earlier examples, however, Peter Lombard was not only exonerated by the Papacy, but was actually endorsed. At Lateran IV, as we shall see, the Papacy confessed *cum petro*, with Peter. Prior to Lombard, Abelard had isolated points of doctrinal contradiction in his *Sic et Non* and suggested that dialectic might be an appropriate means of solving these contradictions. Peter Lombard went one step further and tried to broker the solutions. In his work he attempted to create theologically novel responses that resolved differences in the Christian tradition. Given this totalising dialectical ambition, the *Sententiae* was something of a lightning rod for criticism. In particular, its Christology came under question. As part of Peter Lombard's synthetic project, he needed to inquire as to the constitution of Christ's personhood in order to reconcile contradictory accounts of his identity. The Council of Chalcedon had declared, in 451, that Christ was one person in two natures. He was the second person of the Trinity, composed of mutually imbricated human and divine natures. According to this formulation, Christ's personhood was constituted only in the particular combination of human and divine natures that characterised His Incarnation. This idea of personhood, of course, was very different from the usual definition of the term as it was applicable only to Christ. Boethius, in a formulation which was standard throughout the schools of Paris, had defined a person as an individual substance of a rational nature. According to Boethius, the key characteristics, then, of personhood were individuality and rationality. If the Boethian definition was followed, this would mean that what made a human a person was not the same as that which made Christ a person. Christ's personhood was constituted in his two natures, man's personhood was found in his rational nature. Doctrinally, Christ needed to be fully human to bring about the salvation of humanity, to make satisfactory reparation for the sins of Adam. Yet, how could He be fully human if His personhood was defined differently from that of humans? This was precisely the sort of contradiction that Lombard wanted to resolve in the *Sententiae*. Both the formulation of Chalcedon and the doctrinal writings of Boethius were considered to be orthodox and authoritative in the Christian tradition. How might they be made consistent with each other? Following this problem, Peter Lombard asked whether 'Christ, insofar

---

[9] For a general introduction to the historiography of intellectual heresy between 1050 and 1150 see Southern (1995; 2001), Fichtenau (1992), and Le Goff (1985).

as He is a human being, [was] a person or something else [*aliquid*]?'.[10] This question, and Lombard's answer to it, was the source of charges of Christological Nihilism made against him in the second half of the twelfth century. For, in his answer, Lombard was forced into equations of Christ's being that attempted to define how his being might be broken down and understood in binary terms. The point of the Christological mystery was the irreducibility of the *hypostasis*. Hence, a theologian would invariably fall into error when he tried to reduce Christ to the sum of His parts. It was charged, then, that Lombard said that Christ's human person was not something, or, in fact, nothing at all. He tried to argue that Christ could have a human nature, without having human person. He attempted to follow Chalcedon to the letter, with the result that he refused the idea of Christ's human person, he said that it was an *aliquid*/something else. Consequently, Peter Lombard and his followers were called *Nichilianistae* by their critics – in the first usage of this word. So controversial was he considered to be that he warranted the creation of a neologism, the word that we now know as 'nihilist'.

Once the issue had been raised, it necessitated analysis and resolution because the issue of Christ's nature was the fundamental issue of Christianity itself. Christ's Incarnation and Resurrection was that which enabled the supercession of Jewish Law and that which facilitated human salvation through the intervention of grace. Part of this intervention of grace was the Word that infused all words. After the rupture of the garden, where knowledge was lost, Christ's participation on earth had revitalised signification. Words were no longer vessels for the Law, but living sites of revelation for Christian believers. And the Church held the monopoly on the provision of this Grace. Christ had given Peter the task of founding a church; this authority was passed on from pope to pope, but always with the original petrine dispensation in mind. Christ's constitution of human and divine concomitantly was, obviously, the cornerstone of Christian identity. To be called Christological Nihilist/*Nichilianistae* was not just to be accused of ordinary error. It was to be charged with denying the basis of the linguistic, epistemological, mystical, sacramental and ecclesiastical life of Christendom.

The other serious charge levelled against Peter Lombard, and one that is heard at Lateran IV, was that in his effort to describe the unity of the Trinity he actually created a heretical quaternity. These allegations were made by the apocalyptic monk Joachim of Fiore, who had insisted that the unity of the Trinity be understood as 'a collective and analogous unity in the way many men are called one people and many believers one church'.[11] Joachim's emphasis was on the mystical union of the Trinity.[12] He believed that any attempt to isolate the element that united the three members of the Trinity in a concrete linguistic form would be tantamount to heresy. Joachim argued

---

[10] Peter Lombard (1971–1981: 72): 'An Christus secundum quod homo est sit persona vel aliquid'. Translated in Rosemann (2004: 131).

[11] Alberigo (1972: 231): 'sed quasi collectivam et similitudinarium esse fatetur, quemadmodum dicuntur multi homines unus populus, et multi fideles una ecclesia'. Translated in Rothwell (1975: 644).

[12] On Joachim see Reeves (1969), Wendelborn (1974), Daniel (1980), and Mottu (1977).

that Peter Lombard insisted on the imposition of a conceptual *summa quaedam res* ('a certain highest thing') upon the miraculous diversity of God. That is, Peter Lombard had used this term to designate the quality or thing which links the divine members of the Trinity to each other. Joachim, however, wanted to approach the unity and distinctions between divine things in an always deferred and metaphorical way. To define, in a positive sense, just what that unity consisted of would be too bald and too presumptuous. Rather, the believer should approach divine unity through the comparative structure of analogue. Joachim, throughout his writings, used the visible world as a meditative map for the invisible. He registered chains of spiritual similarity that aimed at a mystical appreciation of God's being. The Council was firm in its condemnation of Joachim's doctrine of 'collective or analogous' Trinitarian unity. The second constitution declared that 'we, with the approbation of the holy and universal Council, believe and confess with Peter [Lombard] that there is one single supreme reality, incomprehensible indeed and ineffable, who truly is Father, Son and Holy Ghost, the three persons together and each of them separately, and therefore in God there is a Trinity only, not a quaternity'.[13] Peter Lombard's *summa quaedam res* was endorsed as the appropriate name for 'the principle of all things, apart from which another cannot be found'.[14] Evidently, Joachim's perceived criticism that the *summa quaedam res* suggested a fourth member of the Trinity held no sway with the Council.

Against Joachim's analogical orientation, the Council pointedly supported Peter Lombard's verbal formulation. In so doing, by drawing stark lines, they clearly legitimised Peter Lombard's technical and conceptual project. It was clearly better, the constitutions inferred, to think about God in terms of discrete categories produced in language, than to assume the confluence of God and Man through the process of imagination and prayer. The second constitution asserted that 'between the Creator and a creature there can be remarked no similarity so great that a greater dissimilarity cannot be seen between them'.[15] Joachim had overstated the similarity between man and God in his conviction that analogy could function as a meditative bridge to the divine. The Council asserted that it was better to err on the side of the principle of dissimilarity, to keep statements about God firmly in the realm of what could be said in absolute faith and in absolute certainty.

The genealogy of the language of Lateran IV is complicated, as my elaboration has shown. The detail is important, however, as it shows that an

---

[13] Alberigo (1972: 232): 'Nos autem, sacro et universali concilio approbante, credimus et confitemur cum Petro, quod una quaedam summa res est, incomprehensibilis quidem et ineffabilis, quae veraciter est Pater et Filius et Spiritus Sanctus, tres simul personae ac sigillatim quaelibet earundum, et ideo in Deo Trinitas est solummodo non quaternitas'. Translated in Rothwell (1975: 644).

[14] Alberigo (1972: 232): 'quae sola est universorum principium, praeter quod aliud inveniri non potest'. Translated in Rothwell (1975: 644).

[15] Alberigo (1972: 232): 'quia inter creatorem et creaturam non potest tanta similitudo notari, quin inter eos maior sit dissimilitudo notanda'. Translated in Rothwell (1975: 645).

assuredness of Roman Catholicism as the glue of Christendom did not necessarily produce a politicised discourse of amities and enmities. Instead, the desire of the Council to state the boundaries of orthodoxy was embedded in a concomitant avowal of the limitations of human knowledge of Truth. Yes, the papacy was assured of its original apostolic mandate. As we have seen, the Council confessed *cum petro*, with Peter. But this confession, at this point, is a double edged sword. In confessing thus, the papacy made a playful pun on the names of Peter Lombard and St Peter, on whose rock the church was built.[16] For it was the *summa quaedam res* that was confessed *cum petro*. Peter Lombard's *summa quaedam res* was the name for the principle that the members of the Trinity were somehow linked. It was a notional designation, not an absolute one. Confessing *cum petro* as to the utility and orthodoxy of this demarcation, the Council was to jokily declare this notionality a new rock, and Peter Lombard a new founder. On the back of accusations that the *sprachlogik* of the schools implied an anti-foundational christological nihilism, the words of the papacy declared the opposite. The second constitution of Lateran IV argued that it was precisely when language could be understood as radically estranged from God, as governed by a principle of dissimilarity, that it could be foundational for a positive human epistemology of concepts and distinctions.

The papacy, as an institution, outlined its own sovereign claims via its defence of Peter Lombard. And its 'exception', in Schmittian terms, was not the miracle. It was the petrine dispensation which is continual throughout history in the operations of the sacraments mediated by the clergy. The assuredness of that dispensation enabled Innocent III's papacy to demarcate the exclusive management of presence in the world as the provision of the papacy, and to likewise carve out a separate sphere of productive human notional knowledge. The analogue between exception and miracle depends on a shared suspension of normal laws, of the insertion of the extrinsic and otherwise authorised power. The petrine dispensation and its sacramental function is the normal law, on the other hand, and requires no suspension. The 'exception', in this instance, is entirely unexceptional. Rather, the petrine dispensation is expressly foundational and literally legitimising. According to the logic of Lateran IV, then, it is the exception that decides the sovereign.

It seems to me, then, that Lateran IV does proffer a theologically neutralised political language. It does this by disavowing positive affirmations of God's being, and insisting on the fundamental contingency of language. Schmitt's charge had been that the evacuation of theology from political formulations was a consequence of the enforced religious relativism of the Reformation, and the need to find a political language by which this might be accommodated. As the example of Lateran IV shows, however, Schmitt's historical schema is reductive and excessively foundational. Schmitt posits a pre-lapsarian ideal politics of the medieval, which is ruptured by the fall of the reformation. But it seems that the Council of 1215 – in spite of its

---

[16] In Tanner (1990) *cum petro*, in this context, is translated as 'with Peter Lombard'. An anonymous late thirteenth century treatise against Peter Lombard also reads *cum petro* as 'with Peter Lombard'. See Ottaviano (1934).

universalising desires – registered the impossibility of articulating a completely sacralised political sphere. In fact, it argued for the opposite.

The problem of articulating a clear political agenda at Lateran IV resides in an explicit acknowledgement of the limitations of human language as a conduit for the expression of truth. For medieval thinkers like Peter Lombard, language always inclines towards the divine and yet stays firmly limited in its creaturely context. The same tension, I think, can be seen in Schmitt's reading of political theology. It reveals a desire to formalise historically particular distinctions, such as those between friends and enemies, into an absolute theory of politics. It is an abstraction, perversely, that claims to be ground in the earth. Derrida writes of Schmitt's capacity 'to count on the pure impurity, on the impure purity of the political as such, of the properly political' (Derrida 1997: 116). Schmitt's particular contribution, as Derrida points out in the *Politics of Friendship*, is the exposition of a political concept that registers both the ideality of politics – its inclination towards perfection – as well as its foundation in concrete enmity. But this articulation of the concrete as foundational runs the risk of becoming itself an illusory chimera. As Derrida points out 'But no politics has ever been adequate to its concept. No political event can be correctly described or defined with recourse to these concepts. And this inadequation is not accidental, since politics is essentially a *praxis*' (Derrida 1997: 114).

In light of my own and Derrida's reading of Schmitt, Lateran IV registers as a historically situated negotiation of the *aporia* of politics and thinking politically. The radical statement of dissimilarity between Man and God of Lateran IV provides a notion of the political that is necessarily neutralised and evacuated of theological portent. In spite of the originating petrine dispensation that guarantees sovereign authority, the papacy declares a mode to the separation of politics from the Divine. It does this by casting language and events in the creaturely world as irreparably estranged from God. Language and history, then, conform to human logic and must be understood as coherent in those terms. The problem of the pure impurity of the political is not one that belongs to modernity alone, and neither does the neutralising strategy of its management. Instead, as Derrida points out, the condition of the political is defined by the impossibility of the merging of the action and ideal: 'the concrete finally remains, in its purity, out of reach' (Derrida 1997: 117).

References

Agamben, G. 1998. *Homo Sacer: Sovereign Power and Bare Life.* Translated by D. Heller-Roazen. Stanford, CA: Stanford University Press.

Agamben, G. 2005. *State of Exception.* Translated by K. Attell. Chicago, IL: University of Chicago Press.

Alberigo, J. 1972. *Conciliorum Oecumenicorum Decreta.* Bologna: Instituto Per Le Scienze Religiose.

Colish, M. 1994. *Peter Lombard.* Leiden: Brill.

Daniel, E. R. 1980. 'The Double Procession of the Holy Spirit in Joachim of Fiore's Understanding of History'. *Speculum* 55, 469–83.

Derrida, J. 1989. 'How to Avoid Speaking: Denials'. Translated by K. Frieden. In S. Budick and W. Iser (eds), *Languages of the Unsayable.* New York: Columbia University Press, 3–70.

Derrida, J. 1997. *The Politics of Friendship*. Translated by G. Collins. London: Verso.

Fichtenau, H. 1992. *Ketzer und Professoren: Häresie und Vernunftglaube im Hochmittelalter*. Munich: Verlag C. H. Beck.

Le Goff, J. 1985. *Les intellectuels au Moyen Âge*. Paris: Seuil.

Lombard, P. 1971–1981. *Sententiae in IV libris distinctae*. Edited by I. Brady, O.F.M in two volumes. Grottaferrata: Editiones Collegii S. Bonaventurae Ad Claras Acquas.

Marion, J.-L. 2002. *In Excess*. Translated by R. Horner. New York: Fordham University Press.

McCormick, J. P. 1998. 'Political Theory and Political Theology: The Second Wave of Carl Schmitt in English'. *Political Theory* 26, 830–54.

Mews, C. J. and Monagle, C. 2010. 'Peter Lombard, Joachim of Fiore, and the Fourth Lateran Council', forthcoming in *Medioevo*.

Milem, B. 2007. 'Four Theories of Negative Theology'. *The Heythrop Journal* 48, 187–204.

Mottu, H. 1977. *La Manifestation de l'Esprit selon Joachim de Fiore*. Paris: Labor & Fides.

Mouffe, C. 1999. *The Challenge of Carl Schmitt*. London: Verso.

Mouffe, C. 2000. *The Democratic Paradox*, London: Verso.

Ottaviano, C. 1934 . *Joachimi abbatis Liber contra Lombardum (Scuola di Gioacchino da Fiore)*. Rome: Reale Accademia d'Italia.

Reeves, M. 1969. *The Influence of Prophecy in the later Middle Ages*. Oxford: Clarendon Press.

Robb, F. 1997. 'The Fourth Lateran Council's Definition of Trinitarian Orthodoxy'. *Journal of Ecclesiastical History* 48, 22–43.

Roseman, P. 2004. *Peter Lombard*. Oxford: Oxford University Press.

Rothwell, H. 1975. *English Historical Documents: 1189–1327*. New York: Oxford University Press.

Schmitt, C. 1976. *The Concept of the Political*. Translated by G. D. Schwab. New Brunswick: Rutgers University.

Schmitt, C. 1985. *Political Theology: Four Chapters on the Concept of Sovereignty*. Translated by G. D. Schwab. Cambridge, MA: MIT Press.

Schmitt, C. 1993. 'The Age of Neutralizations and Depoliticizations'. Translated by M. Konzell and J. E. McCormick. *Telos* 96, 130–42.

Schmitt, C. 1996. *Roman Catholicism and Political Form*. Translated by G. L. Ulmen. Westport, CT: Greenwood Press.

Southern, R. 1995 and 2001. *Scholastic Humanism and the Unification of Europe*. Two volumes. Oxford: Blackwell.

Tanner, N. 1990. *Decrees of the Ecumenical Councils*. London: Sheed & Ward.

Thompson, A. 2005. 'The Spectrality of Politics'. In *Deconstruction and Democracy: Derrida's Politics of Friendship*. London: Continuum, 148–60.

Wendelborn, G. 1974. *Gott und Geschichte: Joachim von Fiore und die Hoffnung der Christenheit*. Vienna: Bohlau.

Enmity and Culture: The Rhetoric of Political Theology and the Exception in Carl Schmitt

Jürgen Fohrmann and (Translated by Dimitris Vardoulakis)

Abstract *This article compares Carl Schmitt's and Walter Benjamin's discussion of the figure of Hamlet. This comparison evaluates Schmitt's response in* Hamlet or Hecuba *to Benjamin's discussion of the 'exception' in* Origins of the German Tragic Drama. *'Deciding upon the exception' is a defining characteristic of sovereignty, so that the comparison between Schmitt and Benjamin is also an evaluation of their respective theories of sovereignty. It will appear that the notion of the aesthetic is crucial in understanding this constellation of ideas.*

1. The state of emergency[1]

In the relationship between violence and law [*Recht*], the discussion of sovereignty will be one of the central issues at stake. The cultural determination of sovereignty, as well as its medium, are closely interwoven with the theory of the state of emergency. The problem is one of the status of the state of emergency in relation to the state of exception: can emergency be taken as a permanent state, or can it be considered in a different way? From this perspective, Walter Benjamin's melancholic ruler in *The Origins of the German Tragic Drama* necessarily presents a challenge to the pre-eminent thinker of the state of emergency and the power of the decision, Carl Schmitt. Such a challenge calls for investigation. To do so, I will concentrate on Schmitt's reply to Benjamin,

---

[1] Translator's note: The word 'Enstfall' has been rendered throughout as 'state of emergency' while the 'Ausnahmezustand' has become 'state of exception'. (The only exception is the subtitle, where 'Ausnahmezustand' has been translated as 'exception' for brevity.) In general, 'Erstfall' refers to a situation of emergency which gives rises to (or causes) a suspension of law or a 'martial law'. This suspension is referred to in German legal terminology as 'Ausnahmezustand'. The first sentence of Carl Schmitt's *Political Theology* defines sovereignty thus: 'The sovereign is he who decides on the exception [*Ausnahmezustand*]'. However, Schmitt frequently uses the two terms interchangeably. The translator would like to thank Patrizia Hucke and Clare Monagle, as well as Professor Jürgen Fohrmann, for commenting on earlier drafts.

carried out after Benjamin's death.[2] I will turn initially to a work that, despite seeming peripheral to these questions, in matter of fact concerns the central issues of *political theology*.[3] This work is Schmitt's *Hamlet or Hecuba*. Schmitt in *Hamlet or Hecuba: The Incursion of Time in Play* from 1956, is reliant upon 'play' – in the figurative meaning of the word. The question is whether it is possible to suspend the state of emergency. For Schmitt , this means 'to deal with it [i.e. the emergency] playfully in an artwork that is understood as play'. The answer to this question is developed with reference to Shakespeare's *Hamlet*, which forms the background of the renewed confrontation with Benjamin's *German Tragic Drama*. In *German Tragic Drama*, Benjamin had essentially agreed with Schmitt's *Political Theology*, and 'in 1930 expressed his thanks in a personal letter' to Schmitt (Schmitt 1956: 64). Nonetheless, essential positions of the *German Tragic Drama* contradict, even subvert, Schmitt's concepts and, in 1956, Schmitt recommences his conversation with the then-deceased Benjamin.

In brief, what does Schmitt's work deal with? With the rejection of either a psychological or a historical exegesis of *Hamlet*, which also aims to 'eliminate the prejudices of a romantic aesthetic', Schmitt places at centre stage the curious relationship between Hamlet and his mother, whose possible complicity in the murder of her husband as well as her marriage to the murderer remain, in substance, unspeakable for Hamlet (Schmitt 1956: 70). Such silence, for Shakespeare, had nothing to do with 'sparing the ladies', he was not concerned with a 'lady cult' (Schmitt 1956: 18; we will return later to the 'lady cult'). Rather, this impermissibility of speaking about the guilt of the mother is the ascription of a concrete historical taboo, says Schmitt, 'and I can identify this concrete taboo' (Schmitt 1956: 18). Here, Schmitt offers an historical explanation. The figure of Hamlet was once identified with the son of Mary Stuart – Hamlet represents James I of England. Schmitt adumbrates that Mary Stuart had also married the murderer of her husband. And, in his struggle for the English throne, James was torn between Catholicism and Protestantism, with no desire to see the burden of a murder in his own genealogy. The majority would have known, or at least guessed at, the mother's complicity in the murder. Schmitt notes that Shakespeare was a follower of the Earl of Essex who was the second character of force behind Hamlet. This Earl of Essex, who was murdered in 1601, was in his turn a follower of James I of England. Between 1600 and 1603, the years during which *Hamlet* was written, Shakespeare himself was affected by the arguments concerning the

---

[2] The relation between Walter Benjamin and Carl Schmitt requires a whole article. If one wanted to determine more clearly the relation, the contrasting texts – to name only the most significant ones – would have been, on the one hand, Schmitt's *Political Romanticism* (1919) and Benjamin's *The Concept of Criticism in German Romanticism* (submitted as a dissertation in 1919 and published in 1920), and, on the other hand, Schmitt's *Political Theology* (1922) and Benjamin's *The Origin of German Tragic Drama* (submitted as an habilitation in 1925, published in 1928).

[3] I refrain here from defining 'political theology', since it will progressively unfold as a concept in the development of the argument. For the role of transcendence in Schmitt, see Meuter (1991).

succession of Elizabeth to the English throne. Schmitt underscores the consequences of these circumstances:

> In respect of James, the son of Mary Stuart, the King in waiting, it was impossible to impute the guilt of a mother in the murder of the father. Nevertheless the audience [*Publikum*] of *Hamlet*, just like the whole of protestant England and in particular London, were entirely convinced of Mary Stuart's guilt. In respect of the English public [*Publikum*] it was altogether impossible to impute the innocence of the mother. The issue of guilt, therefore, had to be dealt with carefully. The action of *Hamlet* was, as a consequence, unclear and restrained. (Schmitt 1956: 21)

There appear to be two taboos that Shakespeare was trying to play with: the 'taboo of the queen' and the taboo of the avenger. The figure of the avenger, however, can be sidestepped in favour of 'a melancholic who becomes restrained through reflection' (Schmitt 1956: 22). This is what constitutes for Schmitt 'the "Hamletization" of the avenger' (Schmitt 1956: 24). The play was surely a play, but under the play's stage, 'through the masks and costumes, shimmered a frightening historical reality' (Schmitt 1956: 21).

So far so good. But what is the importance of this argument in Schmitt's subsequent elaborations? There is a scene in *Hamlet* that works for Schmitt like a cipher and functions as a motto to his book. It is from the 1603 text of *Hamlet* Act 2 Scene 2. The speaker is Hamlet:

> Why these Players here draw water from eyes:
> For Hecuba,
> why what is Hecuba to him, or he to Hecuba?
> What would he do and if he had my losse?
> His father murdred, and a Crowne bereft him.

Let us situate, briefly, this scene within the context of the play: Hamlet asks an actor from the city's theatre, who was in fact employed by his mother and the new king, to cheer him up by reciting a scene that announces the death of Priamos and depicts the reaction of Hecuba, his wife. The scene has a certain parallel to the situation in the Danish court – it contains the slaying of the king and the reaction from the queen. It thereby functions as the first play within a play, whose purpose is to measure the intensity of Hamlet's own feelings, and also to anticipate the emotional reaction caused by the putative murder. Here, Schmitt takes this play within a play as Hamlet's meta-commentary upon the whole constellation – 'it is the real theatre play once again in front of the stage' (Schmitt 1956: 45). This is the constellation expressed in *Hamlet*, namely the relationship between the eruption of reality, the emergency in the play, on the one side, and, on the other, the play, which was posing as reality while trying to dominate the real. Hence, the issue is about what is primary – the real or the aesthetic?

Although Hamlet's meta-commentary destroys the illusionary effect of the play, Schmitt observes that it derives an additional value:

This additional value resides in the objective reality of the tragic happening itself, in the enigmatic link and enmeshment of incontestably real people in the incalculable progression of incontestably real events. The impossibility to deconstruct and relativize the seriousness of the tragic happening is based on this reality. As a result, this seriousness cannot be playfully gambled away ... The unmovable reality is the silent rock upon which the play breaks and the surf of the properly tragic foams. This is the last and insurmountable limit of free poetic invention. A poet wants and ought to invent a lot, but he cannot invent the core of reality within the tragic action. We can cry about Hecuba, one can cry about all sorts of things, a lot is sad, but the tragic arises primarily out of a happening taken as the insurmountably real for all concerned – the poet, the actor and the audience. (Schmitt 1956: 47)

The point of this pronouncement becomes clear when it is understood that it enables Schmitt to tackle anew a contrast that was important in Benjamin's *German Tragic Drama*: the contrast between tragedy and baroque theatre or *Trauerspiel*:

Historical life, as it was conceived at that time, is its [the *Trauerspiel*'s] content, its true object. In this it is different from tragedy. For the object of the latter is not history by myth, and the tragic stature of the *dramatis personae* does not derive from rank – the absolute monarchy – but from the prehistoric epoch of their existence – the past ages of heroes. (Benjamin 2003: 62)

This link between *Trauerspiel* and historical life, and also between tragedy and myth, which Benjamin took up, are outlined in the following statement – which perhaps echoes ideas found in Walter Benjamin's essay 'Fate and Character': 'The religious man of the baroque era clings so tightly to the world because of the feeling that he is being driven along to a cataract with it. The baroque knows no eschatology' (Benjamin 2003: 66). The historical life unfolding in baroque is, then, strictly immanent. In it, the sovereign has the most central position. The reason is that it is incumbent upon him – here Benjamin seizes upon Schmitt's idea – to end the (religious) civil war as a continuing state of exception. This he accomplishes through the usurpation of power, which is simultaneously the way the sovereign is determined. 'The sovereign is the representative of history. He holds the course of history in his hand like a scepter'. And on the same page: 'Whereas the modern concept of sovereignty amounts to a supreme executive power on the part of the prince, the baroque concept emerges from a discussion of the state of exception, and makes it the most important function of the prince to aver this. The ruler is designated from the outset as the holder of dictatorial power if war, revolt, or other catastrophes should lead to a state of exception' (Benjamin 2003: 65).

Two references are noticeable here initially. Firstly, there is no longer a theological interpretation of the catastrophe in Benjamin's understanding of the baroque but, rather, the catastrophe is immanent. For this reason, the displacement of transcendence suspends the most important condition for religious apocalyptic discourse. Because it is only in the apocalypse that the catastrophe is fulfilled as part of a general history of salvation, it is, indeed, the instant in which truth is revealed. Its state of emergency is thoroughly uncircumventable, and thus it is always an occurrence whose possibility is actualised. The omission of eschatology in the baroque must find a functional substitute for the foundational and enforcing place which has been emptied of transcendence. Otherwise the state of exception loses all its meaning. This substitution of transcendence is accomplished in political theology through instantaneity: in the moment, i.e. the moment of the putatively pending catastrophe, the instance of history takes over the functional place of transcendence as ethics, as legitimation and as guideline. This is the instance of activity in the process of usurpation. The activity of the prince accomplishes the state's 'process of the history of salvation' and embodies in the prince the sovereign of the subjects (and thereby an autonomous subject in the modern sense).

What happens, though, if at the same time this sovereign is not a 'modern subject', is not free, is not *legibus solutus*?[4] What happens if the sovereign is instead an old kind of subject, subjected to nature, his own nature, and thereby continuing to exhibit his creatureliness even in his exalted position? Is it not the case, then, that the creature is the representative of other creatures, rather than a subject representing other subjects? As Benjamin showed in his book on *German Tragic Drama*, the import of these questions is a constitutive condition of the *Trauerspiel*'s genre:

> The developing formal language of the *Trauerspiel* can very well be seen as the emergence of the contemplative necessities which are implicit in the contemporary theological situation. One of these, and it is consequent upon the total disappearance of eschatology, is the attempt to find, in a reversion to a bare state of creation, consolation for the renunciation of a state of grace. (Benjamin 2003: 80–81)

The sovereign, as the head of creatures, reverts himself to the deepest creatureliness. It comes down to the distinction between 'the power of the ruler and the capacity to rule' (Benjamin 2003: 70). This leads either to an overabundance of affectivity resulting in frenzy, or adversely, to excessive reflectivity leading to the inability to make a decision. 'The prince, who is responsible for making the decision to proclaim the state of exception, reveals, at the first opportunity, that he is almost incapable of making a decision' (Benjamin 2003: 71). The monarch who corresponds to the situation of the prince takes at once the spirit as 'the capacity to exercise dictatorship', while the melancholy now effecting this capacity develops a fascination out of, and also for, itself (Benjamin 2003: 98). Since a creatureliness should be able to overcome all affects through suicide, the sovereign achieves a depersonalisation that is nothing but the release of the feeling belonging to the

---

4 Translator's note: The Roman law maxim 'princepts legibus solutus est' literally means that 'the prince is not bound by the law' or that the sovereign is above the law.

Trauerspiel. Benjamin observes: 'Mourning [*Trauer*] is the state of mind in which feeling revives the empty world in the form of a mask, and derives an enigmatic satisfaction in contemplating it' (Benjamin 2003: 139). Such mourning was not to be overcome in the German baroque *Trauerspiel*, and there is, in fact, only one instance where this has occurred.

> But Germany was not the country that was able to do this. The figure is Hamlet. The secret of his person is contained within the playful, but for this very reason firmly circumscribed, passage through all the stages in this complex of intentions, just as the secret of his fate is contained in an action which, according to this, his way of looking at things, is perfectly homogeneous. For the *Trauerspiel* Hamlet alone is a spectator by the grace of God; but he cannot find satisfaction in what he sees enacted, only in his own fate. His life, the exemplary object of his mourning, points, before its extinction, to the Christian providence in whose bosom his mournful images are transformed into a blessed existence ... Only Shakespeare was capable of striking Christian sparks from the baroque rigidity of the melancholic, un-stoic as it is un-Christian, pseudo-antique as it is pseudo-pietistic ... It is only in this prince that melancholy self-absorption attains to Christianity. (Benjamin 2003: 157–58)

Schmitt's extrapolation was completely different from that of Benjamin. In order to properly gauge the difference, it is important to remember that the issue at hand for Schmitt is a *political theology* that assumes the task of think-ing the state of emergency as the end of time for the human in connection with a conceivable history of salvation. It is – let it be noted – a theology without eschatology. It desires to and must, therefore, replace the Ultimate Judge with an equivalent. This equivalent, then, is able to form the link between the impossibility of circumventing the emergency and the necessity to act. This forms the condition under which a solution may be found, as conceived by Schmitt.

Schmitt grants that, while he finds Benjamin's citation 'excellent', it remains somewhat obscure to him (Schmitt 1956: 63). In any case, Benjamin appears to him to be wrong. How is this enigmatic passage from Benjamin to be understood? 'Melancholy [is] redeemed by being confronted with itself' (Benjamin 2003: 158). Such confrontation with oneself is an observation of the self, as well as an observation 'with God's grace'. According to Benjamin, Hamlet sees himself; he sees his own play as play and sees the annulment of the play in relation to providence. He is, therefore, in a higher sense, player/actor, participant/partaker, and, it is possible to say, also an observer. His life does not represent only the irrupting reality, but equally his life is a play that regards itself as a play. Not only is there a groundless reflection upon things by the subject, turning this reflection into enigmatic mourning, but also the melancholy regards melancholy as play and sublates it *sub specie aeternitatis*. Benjamin's interpretation would ennoble play. This is not the case with Schmitt's notion of the state of emergency.

The whole of Schmitt's argumentation is directed precisely towards not admitting this position of ennobling play. His arch enemy is romantic aesthetics, in which he perceives the self-realisation of play, 'Schiller incorporated'.[5] This is an aesthetic of the 'amateur [*Heimarbeiter*]' which, for Schmitt, closely related to the hateful 'lady cult' and in general, who would have thought, to 'little kids and naughty kittens play with particular brio' (Schmitt 1956: 41). Therefore, for Schmitt, *Hamlet* is not a *Trauerspiel* at all, but rather, a tragedy. A tragedy which, however, leaves ineradicable traces of reality. The state of emergency glimmers in these traces, and it is shaped by myth. While Benjamin abandoned myth in favour of modernity, Schmitt allows – at least in Hamlet – the origination of a new myth. This myth is based on the uncovering of those already mentioned taboos, the taboo of the queen/mother and the taboo of the avenger, as well as on its consequent, the sidestepping of the revenge taboo. As a result, Schmitt accomplishes a notable displacement. Benjamin's opposing argument about the incapacity for action and the melancholy of the sovereign, which is clearly contrary to Schmitt's theory, is now incorporated into Schmitt's own theory but reconfigured as the sign of new, modern myth. Hamlet's indecision is, according to Schmitt, the condition for the possibility that this myth 'about the implied state of emergency in a veiled history' has arisen, and become the model for many different historical circumstances, such as those of Germany. For Germany is, or has, long been represented by Hamlet. This is because Hamlet stands, according to Schmitt, between the two other modern figures of mythical power, namely between the Catholicism of Don Quixote and the Protestantism of Faust. Since Hamlet is positioned exactly in the middle of this religious split, he may be compared with Germany. It could even be said that Hamlet provides in the 'in-between' a certain unity, and through this develops into myth or expression of 'proper tragedy'. It is not permissible to resolve this 'in-between' in the play of art, and hence playfully gamble it away. But, contends Schmitt, Shakespeare 'shyly' skirts around the taboos in *Hamlet*. He does not gamble them away playfully; rather, he connects them to the problematic of a character, which rewards him with the creation of a new myth.

> The taboo muffling the guilt of the queen and the sidestepping of the character-type of the avenger that has lead to the hamletization of the hero are two shadows, two obscurities. They are not at all mere political or historical implications – they are neither mere allusions [*Anspielungen*] nor true reflection. They are rather actualities that are received in, and respected by, the play. The real play skirts around them. They disturb the purposelessness of the pure play. In so far as they are considered from the perspective of play, they are something negative. But they have effectuated the stage character, Hamlet's, becoming a myth. From this perspective they are something positive, since they have elevated the *Trauerspiel* into a tragedy. (Schmitt 1956: 46)

And I take up here again an extract I have already cited above:

---

[5] Translator's note: English in the original.

This additional value resides in the objective reality of the tragic happening itself, in the enigmatic link and enmeshment of incontestably real people in the incalculable progression of incontestably real events. The impossibility to unconstruct and relativize the seriousness of the tragic happening is based on this reality. As a result this seriousness cannot be playfully gambled away. (Schmitt 1956: 47)

The emphasis lies squarely on the reality. It is in the absolutely foundational position, which is marked linguistically with the negating prefixes 'un-' and 'in-' that Schmitt continuously repeats. In this way, reality assumes the function of a constitutive point. The play as the third, as Schmitt calls it, is, however, the not-serious or that which never leads to an emergency. It is, in the language of John's *Revelations*, 'lukewarm', that is, that which is unforthcoming and wants to effectuate an erosion of seriousness and emergency. Consequently, Schmitt concentrates on opposing that 'lukewarm', the play, the aesthetic. 'So then because thou art lukewarm, and neither cold nor hot, I will spue thee out of my mouth' (John, *Revelations*, 3.16, King James Version).

2. Political theology

Like in John's *Revelations*, Schmitt also calls for combating the 'lukewarm'. Since *Political Romanticism*, Schmitt had attempted to consolidate the characteristics of such indecision under the description of 'subjective occasionalism'. For Schmitt this means that 'the romantic subject treats the world as an occasion and an opportunity for his romantic productivity' (Schmitt 1986: 17). The subject has usurped the position of God.

Between the point of concrete reality that serves as an incidental occasion and the creative romantic, an interesting, colorful world arises that often has an amazing aesthetic attraction. We can assent to it aesthetically, but taking it seriously in a moral or objective fashion would call for an ironic mode of treatment. (Schmitt 1986: 19)

Romanticism is linked, therefore, according to Schmitt, to the following temporal structure:

Every instant is transformed into a point in a structure. And just as the romantic emotion moves between the compressed ego and the expansion into the cosmos, so every point is a circle at the same time, and every circle a point. The community is an extended individual, the individual a concentrated community. Every historical instant is an elastic point in the vast fantasy of the philosophy of history with which we dispose over peoples and eons. That is the way to guarantee the romantic supremacy over reality. 'All the accidents of our life are material of which we can make whatever we want'. Everything is 'the first term in an infinite series, the beginning of an endless novel' (Novalis). (Schmitt 1986: 74; translation modified)

Schmitt distinguishes between two kind of occasionalism, metaphysical and romantic. The metaphysical implies a 'higher third' (Schmitt 1986: 88), which means that it overcomes the occasional problem of the 'real cause', of the relationship between the particular case and its ground, because these become integrated into a divine instantiation that the human is not able to know (see Schmitt 1986: 85–86). The romantic occasionalism, conversely, thinks of this third as the abstract, un-obtainable other, whose empty negativity would be able to accord with nothing but a kind of 'slide' from one particular case to the next one:

> It is an occasionalism that shifts from one reality to another. For this occasionalism, the 'higher third' factor – which, occasionalistically, necessarily includes something that is remote, alien, and other – shifts to the other or the alien as such in the continual deflection of another domain. And finally, when the traditional idea of God collapses, the other and the alien become one with the true and the higher. Romanticism is consummated only under this condition. (Schmitt 1986: 91)[6]

This, however, not only transforms 'reality' into an unending sequence of constructions, making it 'unreal'; in addition, it makes the political impossible in Schmitt's definition He famously wrote: 'The specific political distinction to which political actions and motives can be reduced is that between friend and enemy' (Schmitt 1996a: 26).Without it being possible to draw here on the exact argumentation of *The Concept of the Political* (1932), one point must be briefly mentioned, namely that, as Derrida correctly notes, Schmitt's concept of the political is based upon the enemy, not the friend (Derrida 1997: 138). Thus, the political is conceived as a *sui generis* decision, which is the reason it is untraceable onto something else. If one wishes to summarise the core of Schmitt's work, it could be said that an attempt is being made to understand this decision between friend and enemy as that which provides the 'standard' for the entire life, because 'by virtue of this power over the physical life of men, the political community transcends all other associations of societies' (Schmitt 1996a: 47). For this to be achieved, the difference between friend and enemy must manifest not only the basis of politics, but rather, it also must be made clear that all reality is related to politics and for this reason – and despite contrary conceptions – reality is, ultimately, always determined by politics. Such politics often elude analysis, being seemingly non-political:

> We have come to recognize that the political is the total, and as a result we know that any decision about whether something is *unpolitical* is always a *political* decision, irrespective of who decides and what reasons are advanced. This also holds for the question whether a particular theology is a political or an unpolitical theology. (Schmitt 1985: 2)

---

[6] See also Balke's (1996) subtle analysis of *causa* and *occasion*.

And this applies also – and particularly – to those areas that appear to elude this reality, for instance, art.

Because art should be the expression of the 'tragic proper', it takes a form that owes its features to the dread of reality. The tragic arises out of every horror that is understood as the 'authentic' perspective of reality. Compared with this horror, the form of tragic art is transparent; it screens and simultaneously transmits 'shy missives' from this horror. The aesthetic should not, therefore, revert to the romantic pretensions of autonomy. On the contrary, if it were to recognise the 'priority' of the state of emergency, then it would no longer appear as inconsequential or harmless. The aesthetic, too, must not be 'lukewarm' and Schmitt – for no one else could do it better than him – articulates succinctly its transcendental principle in *Hamlet oder Hecuba*: true art arises from dread.

A self-effacing aesthetic is, in effect, a product of liberalism – and vice versa. The reason is that 'The distinctive character of romantic occasionalism is that it subjectifies the main factor of the occasionalist system: God. In the liberal bourgeois world, the detached, isolated, and emancipated individual becomes the middle point, the court of last resort, the absolute' (Schmitt 1986: 99). Thus the general inference from the whole *Political Romanticism* is that the specified enemy of Schmitt is economic liberalism (see Schmitt 1996b).

This uncirumventability and, at the same time, the dominance of the political, has its source in a – conscious or unconscious – archaic opinion that couples virility and *nomos* and hence, not without reason, it finds its best elaboration in Schmitt's favourable consideration of the partisan. The partisan is he who never lays a claim to 'nurture', but rather he becomes in history the representative of 'the absolute enemy' (see Schmitt 1975).[7] The reason is that 'nomos' means for Schmitt taking [*nehmen*] (from the Greek verb *nemein*), appropriation [*Nahme*] and parts. This is the dividing of that which is taken and finally the utilisation of this appropriation (see Schmitt 2003).[8] And so at the end politics denotes 'divisions' and its constellations are the friend and the enemy.

However, in order to represent his position, Schmitt requires his own theory of politics – a politics opposed to false aestheticisation, political and economic liberalism. This is a politics whose own theory marks the enemy. And this enemy is not a military opponent; rather the political constitutes itself in opposition precisely to those who abrogate the schema of 'friend versus enemy'. This is, then, a fight against those who are 'lukewarm' – that is, those who could also be described as remaining uncommitted and who are

---

[7] Translator's note: Schmitt derives the constitutive relation between nurture or *Hegung* and the law or *nomos* through a reference to Jost Tier's 'Zaun und Mannring' (1942) – see Schmitt (2003: 75), translation modified.

[8] Translator's note: The author here uses Schmitt's interplay of the Greek verb *nemein* (meaning primarily to take, but it is also the root for the word *nomos* or law) and German words 'nehmen' (to take), 'Nahme' (seizure, commonly used as a compound, e.g. 'Landnahme' meaning land appropriation) and 'das Genommene' (that which is taken). This interplay between words is impossible to retain in English. See Schmitt's article 'Nomos – Nahme – Name', translated in Schmitt (2003: 336–50).

for this reason intellectual protractors.[9] It is only in this way that the end of Schmitt's own discourse can be maintained, namely the perpetuating of binarism at all cost, the dominance of politics. Its arch enemy is called: the (romantic) third.

I allow myself here to make what I regard as a political footnote. Such an attempt to mortify the third also characterises anti-Semitic arguments. This could be shown in detail, for instance, by reading Eugen Dühring's *The Jewish Question as a Racial, Moral, and Cultural Question: With a World-historical Answer* from 1881. I mention here briefly only the following. According to that which Dühring framed as an uncircumventable and substantiated argumentation, the 'Jew' was attributed first of all the intentionally third character: the 'Jew' was the character that associated with neither the one nor the other side, pursuing instead its 'self-interested affairs' with both sides. For Dühring, then, the 'Jew' represents everything that is beyond culture, since culture presupposes for him a stable identity that can mark out its opposites, something that can allow for different parties. 'The Jew exploits consistently the spirit as well as the good of others' (Dühring 1881: 77). He is 'socially inept' (Dühring 1881: 94). Consequently, he threatens not just every single nationality, but humanity as a whole. In other words, the 'Jew' represents – hurrying to conclude with Dühring's cynical arguments – 'the choice to exploit all peoples, that is, the enemy of mankind. A religion adverse to humanity cannot be tolerant. It can only destroy and oppress ... there is no third' (Dühring 1881: 97). Where corruption dominates, the Jews are the corruption of corruption (see Dühring 1881: 7–8). And by postulating already in the 1880s that the 'Jewish' is 'an internal Cartago' of humanity, Dühring demanded the consequences that the national socialists should have later realised (Dühring 1881: 157).

I do not want to pursue this parallel but, instead, I will attempt to form a systematic argument. The political, under the terms of such a discourse, presupposes the construction of a non-political third that is 'real' and that, even though it wants to evade the schema of 'friend versus enemy', is nevertheless integrated with it. And here, also, the state of emergency dominates. No third is to be permitted because the discourse of political theology only legitimates itself through the availability of such a putative third, anything that allows for a political theology can be taken for such a third in order to be negated. It is easy to see how, in such a line of thought, a structure can be grounded that can be applied (almost) arbitrarily and to (almost) anything (be it in the aesthetic or in the ethical domain). And there is always a threat of not only this or that, but of an (imminent) total demise.

There is a connection, then, between the third party – what in rhetoric and logic is called the excluded middle or *tertium non datur* – with the construction of an absolutely posited enemy under the conditions of urgency. Such a connection grounds not only a religiously motivated apocalyptic

---

[9] This is simultaneously a fight against 'immanent speech'; see on this Brokoff (2001).

discourse, but also political theology as a theology without eschatology.[10] In this way, the 'real reality' assumes the function of transcendence. Behind every banal surface and every instance of play that offers us bad art, lies the archaic force of this reality, its *'nemein'*, which can always emerge as a sudden event. The state of emergency, then, is a transhistorical category, an absolute presence, and the human voice announcing this must make known the moment of transcendence (with a libido of its own) through a particular rhetoric. For how else can one avoid the fact that the enemy is actually a friend, the enemy that I myself am? How else can one avoid – in Theodor Däubler's words cited by Carl Schmitt in *Ex Captivate Salus* – that 'the enemy is our own question as a figure' (Schmitt 1950: 90; see Derrida 1997).[11]

This rhetoric of absolute reality, however, cannot avail itself of any more implanted words, it does not regard itself legitimated as 'real' any longer through a transcendent violence. Thus it opts for another way. Although it is thoroughly metaphorised – one can recall the abundance of images in Schmitt's vocabulary whenever he speaks of the state of emergency – such a rhetoric must nevertheless completely forget the rhetorical status of its words. For it wants to be pure reality. The trace of the impending danger should unmistakably traverse that reality as well as every tragic art. The danger should beget the reality from within itself. Hence this rhetoric paradoxically appears in its *persuasio* as non-rhetoric and so it substitutes the implanted instances of an apocalypse with the fiction of a 'reality as such'. Thus, even though the words employed in this rhetoric are not spoken out of a transcendent position, they should still also effect a compelling transcendent meaning. Rhetoric introduces the argument about urgency. The reader is instructed not to linger but to accelerate the movement of his eyes so as to attain a crescendo of reading. Since all lukewarmness arises from slow reading, then the authentic, the particular worst enemy is that adversary who subverts the transcendent character of apocalyptic speech.

These considerations bring me, once again, to a fundamental reflection about 'political theology'. Apart from all the conceptual digressions that would lead back to the nineteenth century and to anarcho-syndicalism (see Meier 1995), one must also recall Schmitt's famous formulation: 'All significant concepts of the modern theory of the state are secularised theological concepts ... because of their systematic structure, the recognition of which is necessary for a sociological consideration of these concepts. The state of exception in jurisprudence is analogous to the miracle in theology' (Schmitt 1985: 36).[12] That recognition can be linked to the argument Schmitt develops in the same chapter, according to which this secularisation of theological concepts is concerned with 'the politicization of theological concepts', as

---

[10] On a history of the concept 'political theology' and a re-evaluation of the meaning of the theologisation of political concepts see Assmann (2006); see also in the same book Heinrich Meier's introductory comments.

[11] Translator's note: Schmitt has actually slightly changed the citation from Theodor Däubler, who had written 'The enemy is your [*deine*] own question as figure' (1916: 58). Schmitt returns to Däubler's verse – again rendered with the pronoun in the plural – and develops it further, in Schmitt (1975: 88).

[12] About Schmitt see Brokoff (2001: 33) which also contains the relevant literature.

Schmitt puts it in a nutshell (Schmitt 1985: 46). Is it concerned, then, with a rejection of the theorem of secularisation for the modern philosophy of history, something like Karl Löwith's argument that such a philosophy of history essentially presents a secularisation of religion?

It is right to ask whether 'political theology' is interested in or should be interested at all in such historical constructions. Does Schmitt (see Schmitt 2003) think that there is really 'history' beyond his nomos of the earth and his land appropriations and tumultuous oceans? Or is not rather the very point of his approach to have bid farewell once and for all to the philosophy of history? Is he not concerned with the opposite of meaning and history [Sinngeschichten]? Is the aim, rather, to rupture the mythical circulation of the law with an insertion – to recall a thought from Walter Benjamin's 'Critique of Violence' (1997b) – to find an *absolute* point that knows no before or after the power [*Macht*] of the encroaching 'now'? But then this insertion validates neither a juridical rational approach, nor a socialising, pedagogical motivation for action originating from historical optimism. Rather, it validates a radical conception of the political that reverts back to early modern forms of 'political shrewdness' and favours the opportunity (*occasio*). This concept is not interested in the making of laws out of life relations, nor in a semantics of sentiments that often accompanies pacifistic notions. The 'liaisons dangereuses' substitute (again) trust and expectability [*Erwartbarkeit*] in the social (see Choderlos deLaclos, *Liaisons dangereuses* (1782)).

Are not, then, the differences between Löwith's reconstruction of a philosophy of history and its possible (liberal) extrapolations plainly visible? The Schmittian concept of 'political theology' obliterates the teleological horizon and remains altogether uninterested in mediatory forms, whose activation as the telos of history would result in a sort of symmetry between the legitimation of process and that which is 'near'. A liberal theory of the state and the social attempted to propagate such a symmetry in the nineteenth century.

I would not want to pursue this discussion here – as a sort of contribution to 'Schmittian philology'. But the kinship between Schmitt's approach and Löwith's 'eschatological answer' should be stated. However elliptical it may appear, Schmitt's thought shares the presuppositions of the philosophy of history. The reason is that, even though it is not directed towards a particular aim, it still does not want to depart from the figure of a foundation, which incorporates in itself a non-deducible first within a deducible second. This is also only possible through something external, without which the *instant of transcending* would have been impossible. This external element is now inserted into history, bound within in its instantaneity and embodied over and over again. This is the moment of the exception – those points that should be simultaneously a standstill and an actual completion, so that its arising out of decisionism is forgotten in the next step that takes the guise of real action generated from politics. This salvaging of the political, then, should and can therefore – using Schmitt's words – be viewed as analogous to the function of 'the miracle in theology'. This is literally the *incursion* of something external that is uncircumventable, regardless of how much this incursion is theologised or de-theologised – despite Schmitt's Catholicism.[13]

De-theologised: Because in fact one can of course understand the modern state, which has consolidated its structure since the increase of absolutism, as the *legislated power* that put an end to civil war by including – in Giorgio Agamben's (1998) formulation – the 'bare life' as something uncircumventable within the political. Despite that, however, this power must not legitimate itself as theological because its central function is precisely to put an end to the state of exception, to *decide* by *distinguishing* between friend and enemy, by accomplishing an usurpation in order to act and to abandon every hermeneutics of delay – from which Odo Marquard (1989) avers that the state power is seen as remedy to the religious civil war. So the legislated aim is not a hermeneutics, but rather the sovereignty (of the origin) in order not to lose, in the state of emergency, the dimension of the political – the dimension which becomes possible only with the action, the war, even though it is a war only pretending to lead to peace.

In this sense, it is not straightforward to 'simply' repeat a first distinction. On the contrary, the primary positing is always executed anew in the repetition – out of its own force. It is all about, then, the possibility to *decide* upon an *always first distinction* – and this in order not to take as indispensable a conception of the political that holds onto the possibility of the decision when a difference should have been fulfilled. At issue, then, is the *decision* about the *distinction* and thus the suspension of a circulation, of an 'idle chatter', to which this conception of the political always appears as a potential for non-serious play. Schmitt notes this 'circulation', as mentioned earlier, already in political romanticism, whose 'occasionalism' appears to him as an interminable slide from one calculation to the next, and must be clearly distinguished from seizing a political 'opportunity' (see Schmitt 1986: 91). The circulation, then, denotes also a thinking of *iteration* that does not discover a re-production of an origin in repetition, but rather an impure, metonymical, differential movement – and that in the process of the discourse that constantly and quite consciously re-suspends the decision.[14]

Because this conception of the political presupposes the for ever first (and for ever new) distinction, such a politics is concerned with the violence of the 'foundation'. The state of exception, which paradoxically should be at best – at least in discourse – an infinitely distended moment, is itself the time of difference. Or, more precisely, the state of exception serves as the *trope of difference*. The reason is that what is negotiated in the state of exception is the fundamental division between the ability to either decide or not to decide that persists *as the possibility to make a distinction*.

The salvation of life, of physical existence, is 'at play' with the arising of the state of emergency. The inability to reach a decision, then, must be stricken down with authority and the delay must be overcome through action. And this state of emergency is directed towards everything, it lurks and shimmers, to use one of Schmitt's images, whose warm tonality of style is

---

[13] This conception of the outside can be distinguished from Levinas's extrapolation of religion. This point cannot be taken up here. See Levinas (1996).

[14] This recognition is both programmatic and methodological for Derrida, at least since his 'Structure, Sign, and Play in the Discourse of the Human Sciences' (in Derrida 2002).

indicative whenever the state of emergency is discussed. To deny this, that is, is to fail to see the latent possibility of an actualisation. This failure, then, entails for Schmitt that one playfully gambles away the conception of the political. Yet this still does not deduce the incursion. The incursion comes out of Nothing. It does not arise as a metaphor but rather as an abyss, as a *catachresis*.

It is a defining characteristic of political theology to allow this grounding impossibility of distinction to appear over and over again as producing the figure of origin. When the difference between transcendence and difference determines at the same time the scene of the beginning – created in day and night, heaven and earth – then the sovereignty of the origin is the grounding power that will determine all further powers of history or of histories. The origin is sovereign at the point when it becomes elusive as the absolute reference constituting knowledge, as the all-inclusive, as the first before all deferred actions [*Nachträglichen*], so that it is impossible to see it, since it conditions created things. To occupy this position is to make central the question of power. And here we return to the philosophy of history that as always syncopates, allowing it now to find itself in such amplified fantasies of positing, in leaps to positing.

Since the thinking of the first foundation takes the difference between transcendence and immanence as the most fundamental of all distinctions, configuring the entire arrangement, then obviously the assessing of the founding violence is related to a specific *association with the distinction itself*. Thus it is no coincidence that the fundamental speculation about the *sacred* appear at this borderline. Just as the meaning in Latin of *'sacer'* – both holy and accursed – so also the discussion of the sacred is always oriented towards the *drawing of distinctions*.

The place of the 'sacred' is semantically occupied, according to Schmitt, by the ability and the executive power to decide. The instant of the sovereign is the moment degree zero [*Nullmoment*] of history. The reason is that the sacred, just as the decision – as well as everything that resides on the border-line – emerges as a break, as an 'incursion', within which something in-visible *is configured*, something elusive as such. The place of the configuration is the borderline itself that assumes the characteristic of an immediate presence, of an *absolute threshold*.

There are those who, according to Schmitt, want to disguise the serious-ness of the situation whereby any moment can turn into a case of emer-gency. They represent the circular thinking that holds not onto the *occasio*, but rather onto play, the aesthetic, and romantic occasionalism. They want, therefore, to establish the Kingdom of the Lax, which should also be devoid of all alternatives.

The issue, then, is about the uncircumventability of the political *or* the uncircumventability of the aesthetic. The issue pertains to the *binary structure as such*. It is a battle of decisions that the political takes up in the processing of its own conception. It does so in order – through the sharp division between politics and aesthetics – to wage sovereignty and the ability of action against the never disappearing, necessary decisions of infinitely suspending tenden-cies that characterise parliamentarism, liberalism and so on. The division between friend and enemy is, then, according to Schmitt, not so much the worship of different values, but rather the approval or the denial of such a kind of decisionist value creation.

References

Agamben, G. 1998. *Homo Sacer: Sovereign Power and Bare Life.* Translated by D. Heller-Roazen. Stanford, CA: Stanford University Press.

Assmann, J. 2006. *Politische Theologie zwischen Ägypten und Israel.* Munich: Carl Friedrich von Siemens Stiftung.

Balke, F. 1996. *Der Staat nach seinem Ende: Die Versuchung Carl Schmitts.* Munich: Fink.

Benjamin, W. 1997a. 'The Concept of Criticism in German Romanticism'. In M. W. Jennings et al. (eds), *Selected Writings,* volume 1 (pp. 116–200). Cambridge, MA: Belknap, .

Benjamin, W. 1997b. 'Critique of Violence'. In M. W. Jennings et al. (eds), *Selected Writings,* volume 1. Cambridge, MA: Belknap, .

Benjamin, W. 2003. *The Origin of German Tragic Drama.* Translated by J. Osborne. London: Verso.

Brokoff, J. 2001. *Die Apokalypse in der Weimarer Republik.* Munich: Wilhelm Fink.

Däubler, T. 1916. *Hymne an Italien.* Munich: G. Müller.

deLaclos, C. 1782. *Liaisons dangereuses.*

Derrida, J. 1997. *Politics of Friendship.* Translated by G. Collins. Verso: London.

Derrida, J. 2002. *Writing and Difference.* Translated by A. Bass. London: Routledge.

Dühring, E. 1881. *Die Judenfrage als Racen-, Sitten- und Culturfrage: Mit einer weltgeschichtlichen Antwort.* Karlsruhe und Leipzig: Reuter.

Levinas, E. 1996. *Totality and Infinity: An Essay on Exteriority.* Translated by A. Lingis. Pittsburgh: Duquesne University Press.

Marquard, O. 1989. 'The Question, to what Question is Hermeneutics an Answer?'. In *Farewell to Matters of Principle.* Translated by R. M. Wallace. New York: Oxford University Press,

Meier, H. 1995. *Carl Schmitt and Leo Strauss: The Hidden Dialogue.* Translated by H. Lomax. Chicago, IL: University of Chicago Press.

Meuter, G. 1991. 'Zum Begriff der Transzendez bei Carl Schmitt'. *Der Staat* 30, 483–512.

Schmitt, C. 1950. *Ex Captavitate Salus: Erfahrungen der Zeit 1945/47.* Cologne: Greven.

Schmitt, C. 1956. *Hamlet oder Hekuba: Der Einbruch der Zeit in das Spiel.* Düsseldorf and Cologne: Eugen Diederichs.

Schmitt, C. 1975 [1963]. *Theorie des Partisanen: Zwischenbemerkung zum Begriff des Politischen.* Berlin: Duncker & Humblot.

Schmitt, C. 1985. *Political Theology: Four Chapters on the Concept of Sovereignty.* Translated by G. D. Schwab. Cambridge, MA: MIT Press.

Schmitt, C. 1986 [1919]. *Political Romanticism.* Translated by G. Oakes. Cambridge, MA: MIT Press.

Schmitt, C. 1996a. *The Concept of the Political.* Translated by G. D. Schwab. Chicago, IL: University of Chicago Press.

Schmitt, C. 1996b [1925]. *Roman Catholicism and Political Form.* Translated by G. L. Ulmen. Westport, CT: Greenwood Press.

Schmitt, C. 2003. *The Nomos of the Earth in the International Law of the Jus Publicum Europaeum.* Translated by G. L. Ulmen. New York: Telos Press.

The Sovereign Without Domain: Georges Bataille and the Ethics of Nothing

Charles Barbour

There is work on Bataille's part, but it is an effort to escape, an effort to release toward a freedom that is direct.
- Georges Bataille

'Bataille' is *nothing but* a protest against the signification of his own discourse.
- Jean-Luc Nancy

Exception and Transgression

Despite all of the things that might be said to set them apart, including their explicit political commitments, a scattered but consistent critical tradition seeks to associate the work of Georges Bataille with that of Carl Schmitt (for example: Habermas 1990; Jay 1993; Wolin 1996, 2004; Levi 2007). Inasmuch as they both wrote about the sovereign, the argument goes, and associated that figure with a mysterious, quasi-sacred groundlessness or 'nothingness', Bataille and Schmitt formed part of an intellectual milieu or environment that, during the multiple crises of the inter-war period, renounced the project of the Enlightenment, and the achievements of discursive rationality, thus clearing space for and lending credence to the worst excesses of political irrationalism. If the former was a proponent of radical transgression, interested above all else in freedom, and the latter a strict authoritarian, concerned with the establishment and the preservation of political order, this difference, it is believed, only exposes the contradiction inherent to the attack on reason that characterized their age, the reverberations of which continue to shake our own. Thus, according to a logic that is nearly inescapable, not only their similarities hold Bataille and Schmitt together, their differences do as well – as though the only thing placing them in greater proximity to one another than their agreements were their disagreements, or the points at which they effectively diverge.

The first and most obvious purpose of this paper is to take issue with this interpretation of Bataille and Schmitt, and to insist that the differences between these two figures are significant and profound. I argue that, while Bataille's sovereign transgression can only exist within an instant, and can only be sovereign insofar as it remains

37

indifferent to all future purposes or goals, Schmitt's sovereign exception is never so absolute, but motivated from the outset by a return to order, and by a reinvention of the law that it breaks (cf. Geroulanos 2010: 194). For the same reason, and along the same lines, only Bataille endeavours to understand nothingness, or the negativity of the sovereign experience, outside of all relation to positivity, and outside of every dialectic that would afford the sovereign experience a communicable meaning or sense. For Schmitt, on the other hand, the entire logic of the sovereign, and everything that might be understood as an exceptional state, is circumscribed by the problem of political and legal order. To be sure, the exception exceeds the order, but always with the aim of recreating it. And it is justified, albeit retroactively, only insofar as it is able to do so.

Of course, the aforementioned effort to associate Bataille with Schmitt is not merely concerned with textual exegesis. It forms part of a larger attempt to diagnose, and prevent the return of, the political catastrophes of the Twentieth Century. On this line of thought, totalitarianism in general, and fascism in particular, followed from a collapse of civil society, and all of the associations and institutions that come in between the state and the people. Without the mediating influence of civil society, the argument goes, totalitarian political movements were able to combine the boundless enthusiasm of the anomic masses, on the one hand, and the charismatic, personal leadership of a single authority, on the other. They operated by fusing, as it were, the master and the mob. In the absence of public spheres or spaces where individuals could engage in rational deliberation oriented towards consensus, political action was transformed into a terrifying amalgamation of popular fervour and executive fiat – a combination, as some would have it, of Bataille and Schmitt.

While this analysis – which draws on a strong tradition that extends from Alexis de Tocqueville's *Democracy in America* to Hannah Arendt's *Origins of Totalitarianism* – has considerable merits, recent scholarship, such as the work of historical sociologist Dylan Riley, suggests an alternative approach. Without seeking to discredit the Tocquevillian-Arendtian model, Riley notes that, in fact, civil society had *not* collapsed in all of the nations that turned to fascism in the Twentieth Century. Indeed, in Italy, Spain, and Romania, for example, it flourished. Thus, against the tide of what he calls the 'civil society romanticism' of contemporary political theory, or the assumption that the associations that mediate between the state and the people are axiomatically democratic, Riley proposes that, in the inter-war period, '[c]ivil society development *facilitated* the rise of fascism, rather than liberal democracy', and that '[f]ascist movements and regimes grew out of a general crisis of politics, a crisis that itself was a *product* of civil society development' (Riley 2010: 2, emphasis added).

Now, whatever else we might make of the details, we can certainly say that, if this argument, or even something like it, holds, then it will be necessary to rethink a great deal of the dominant understanding of totalitarianism, or mass politics in general, and to reconsider the widely held assumption that there exists a relatively simple opposition between dangerous politics on the one hand and the discursive rationality of the public sphere on the other. Without wanting to exaggerate the issue, and while fully aware that Riley (whose theoretical leanings are more in the direction of Gramsci) would probably take a different approach, it seems to me that a reassessment of Bataille's work could fruitfully inform such a project.

The Ecstasies of Law

I would like to find my way into the question of the differences between Bataille and Schmitt, and the larger relevance of Bataille's work, through a brief consideration of two of the better known efforts to repudiate Bataille by associating him with Schmitt – specifically those of Martin Jay and Richard Wolin. I think the limits of these two interpretations of Bataille reveal something about the strength of Bataille's thought. That is to say, it is exactly what Jay and Wolin misunderstand, or misrepresent, that I would like to privilege and explore. For his part, Jay proposes that there is, if not quite an exact homology, at least a strong family resemblance between Bataille's and Schmitt's respective concepts of sovereignty. But, as I have already begun to suggest, despite the fact that the two thinkers employ the same term, what they mean by sovereignty, and the way that figure operates in their respective texts, is not only discrete, but discrete in important ways. Drawing on similar resources, Wolin insists that both Bataille and the generation of French intellectuals that he influenced (Baudrillard, Derrida, Foucault, and so forth) replace the normative conditions of political action with aesthetic ones, leading to a valorization of transgression for its own sake, or a violent destruction of limits as an end in itself. But while something like this might be at stake, I nevertheless believe that Bataille's project is fundamentally ethical – albeit in a manner that cannot easily be assimilated to a Habermasian, or even Levinasian, conception of ethics.

According to Jay, both Schmitt and Bataille sought 'a revalorization of the concept of sovereignty' in a time of crisis. Lacking what Jay calls 'faith' in 'the power of discursive rationality', and the liberal parliamentary institutions that generally go along with it, both Schmitt and Bataille harboured 'a residual counter-Enlightenment notion of secularized religion' – one related, at least in part, to 'the Catholicism of their youth' (Jay 1993: 50). For Schmitt, this entailed an understanding of sovereignty as the, as it were, external guarantee of political order, and the exceptional, lawless violence required to defend the law. For Bataille, it meant a sovereign experience that exceeds every order, and every effort to limit the will to transgress. But, Jay maintains, these positions amount to two sides of the same coin – a fact evidenced by the fascination that both figures had with fascism, or the sense in which both viewed 'the rise of fascism as a reassertion of the power of sovereignty' against 'the liberal illusion that rational norms or abstract processes of equal exchange could found a polity' (Jay 1993: 57). For Jay, the differences between Schmitt and Bataille are not acute, but integral to the concept of sovereignty they share. That is to say, the concept of sovereignty itself is incoherently split between a will to transgress and a will to order. And for this very reason, Jay concludes, 'rather than being the ground of the political, its ultimate truth revealed in exceptional circumstances', it must ultimately 'share its place with other no less political factors' (Jay 1993: 59).

Although it can certainly be said that Schmitt believes that the sovereign grounds the political, the same is not true of Bataille. Indeed, Bataille begins the third volume of *The Accursed Share*, entitled 'Sovereignty', by insisting that what he means by 'sovereignty ... has little to do with the sovereignty of states, as international law defines it'. Rather, it refers to a 'general ... aspect that is opposed to the servile and the subordinate' (Bataille 1991: 197). While, in the past, some cultures and societies might have latched onto this 'aspect', and organized power structures around it, what actually defines it, or what distinguishes the servile from the sovereign, is not a particular social relation, political position, or legal status, but an experience of time. While it is always servile 'to employ the *present time* for the sake of the *future*', Bataille maintains, it is always sovereign 'to enjoy the present time without having anything else in view but the present time'. Or, to put the same point in different terms, '[l]ife *beyond utility* is the domain of sovereignty' (Bataille 1991: 198).

Despite facile similarities, Schmitt's sovereign has a very different relationship with time. As is well known, Schmitt understands sovereignty in terms of the capacity to decide on the exception, or to decide when it is necessary to break the law in order to preserve or maintain it. But for the same reason, this sovereign is never, like Bataille's, entirely outside of the law, but always inside and outside at once, or on the border or the threshold between law and lawlessness. 'Although [the sovereign] stands outside the normally valid legal system', Schmitt insists, 'he nonetheless belongs to it' (Schmitt 2005: 7). And in this sense, the sovereign's decision is not an absolute negation of order, but the negation of the present order in the name of a future one. One order is broken, we might say, but the principle of order prevails. Or, put differently, each time Schmitt proposes the notion that the sovereign exception exceeds a given legal or political order, he is certain, in an immediately subsequent gesture, to place limits or conditions on that excess. The sovereign exception is always circumscribed in advance by what it is directed towards – namely order.

For example, on Schmitt's account '[w]hat characterizes the exception is principally unlimited authority, which means the suspension of the entire existing order'. But at the same time, Schmitt notes: '[b]ecause the exception is different from anarchy and chaos, order in the juristic sense still prevails even if it is not the ordinary kind' (Schmitt 2005: 12). Or, again: 'Unlike the normal situation, where the autonomous moment of the decision recedes to a minimum, the norm is destroyed in the exception. The exception remains, nevertheless, accessible to jurisprudence because both elements, the norm as well as the decision, remain within the framework of the juristic' (Schmitt 2005: 12-13). So while it is the case that, in the state of exception, executive authority suspends the existing order, and while the decision suspends the norm, from beginning to end, the whole operation is somehow contained by something Schmitt calls 'the juristic'.

The same principle applies to Schmitt's use of theological language, or the discourse of the sacred, to discuss sovereignty. No doubt Schmitt believes that, despite the efforts of the Enlightenment, political theory cannot really do without theological terms. This is why, in the crucial passage in *Political Theology*, he insists that '[a]ll significant concepts in the modern theory of state ... are secularized theological concepts' (Schmitt 2005: 25), and, more specifically, that 'the exception in jurisprudence is akin to the miracle in theology' (Schmitt 2005: 26). At the same time, Schmitt's point is never that human interaction actually is influenced by an unknowable divine entity, or even that some aspect of human existence remains unknowable as such. Rather, his claim is that, from the outset and in every manifestation, theology is always an indirect way of discussing human political relations. What Schmitt calls 'political theology' is always another way of examining political power and political action. For Bataille, on the other hand, the sovereign experience genuinely is a 'nothingness', entirely beyond the register of knowledge in general, and language in particular. And even when we refer to the sovereign experience in terms of the sacred or the divine, we only do so on the condition that we recognize from the outset that we have failed, and that nothing, either directly or indirectly, can actually reference the experience that is at stake.

This brings us back to Schmitt's insistence that, while it breaks with the established order, the sovereign exception nevertheless remains 'accessible to jurisprudence' and 'within the framework of the juristic'. For, along with placing a definite limit on the state of exception, this claim also serves to legitimate or validate Schmitt's own discourse. For if it was the case that the sovereign exception exceeds every order then, by definition, it would also exceed the order of discourse or language – certainly, at any rate, the order of juristic discourse and legal theory. And if that were the case, then Schmitt's own work could only operate or proceed by negating itself. Each argument or claim about the sovereign exception would have to cancel itself out at the point of articulation. And it is this act of self-negation or self-cancelation that Schmitt is not willing to risk. The sovereign exception must remain within the framework of the juristic, for if it did not, then everything Schmitt says about it could only be valid on the condition that it is not valid as well. It could only be true on the condition that it is false. It could only be advanced on the condition that, at the exact same moment and in the exact same gesture, it is also withdrawn, or taken away.

Now, while it seems clear that Schmitt wants to avoid such a paradox of self-negation, it is equally clear that Bataille not only allowed it, but embraced it. Thus, and to pick just one of countless examples, in the third volume of *The Accursed Share*, entitled 'Sovereignty', Bataille highlights the absolute distance between the sovereign experience he wants to discuss, and the language he must use to discuss it. '[K]nowledge is never given to us except by an *unfolding in time*', Bataille writes. It requires 'a *discourse*, which is necessarily deployed in duration' (Bataille 1991: 200). Thus '[t]o know is always to strive, to work'. It is always 'a servile operation, indefinitely resumed, indefinitely repeated'. For this reason, knowledge is 'never sovereign' for 'to be *sovereign* it would have to occur in a moment'. The only way to approximate sovereignty in knowledge, or to approximate some representation of it, would be via something Bataille calls 'unknowing', or by 'cancelling ... every operation of knowledge within ourselves'. It would somehow require a representation of the unrepresentable, or '[t]he miraculous moment when anticipation dissolves into NOTHING, detaching us from the ground on which we were grovelling, in the concatenation of useful activity' (Bataille 1991: 201).

As other commentators have noted, relentlessly producing discourses that operate by cancelling or negating themselves is a – perhaps *the* – defining feature of Bataille's work. As Jean-Luc Nancy puts it, '[a]longside all the themes he deals with, through all the questions and debates, "Bataille" is *nothing but* a protest against the signification of his own discourse' (Nancy 1991: 62). New terms for 'nothingness' are constantly being produced and examined (sovereignty, the sacred, silence, inner experience, communication, intimacy, the heterogeneous, literature, eroticism, nothingness, and so forth), but each one of them is, as it were, rejected as soon as it is deployed, as though it were written down with one hand while being crossed out with the other. Thus, while Schmitt's language is always a veil covering or concealing a deeper intention (a secret that, while opaque, nevertheless remains accessible, at least to those in the know), Bataille's is, instead, a chain of substitutions or supplements for an always already absent origin. As I will argue in the next section of this paper, this practice of writing is not merely rhetorical. It is fundamentally ethical, or fundamental to what I call Bataille's 'ethics of nothing'.

Performing the Unspeakable

Perhaps the most aggressive attempt to posit a link between Schmitt and Bataille is Richard Wolin's 'Left Fascism: Georges Bataille and the German Ideology'. For Wolin, Schmitt and Bataille are both deeply implicated in fascist politics, and they are implicated for similar reasons. At the same time that members of the Frankfurt School were composing a complex, mediated critique of modernity, one that took root in the internal contradictions or dialectic of the Enlightenment, Schmitt and Bataille pursued 'a *total break* with the logic of modernity', and thus 'a totalizing diagnosis of modernity' (Wolin 1996: 409). This approach is revealed most explicitly in their mutual contempt for the modern conception of law. 'Both Schmitt and Bataille view the institution of law as the consummate embodiment of the spirit of bourgeois rationalism', Wolin maintains. 'It symbolizes everything they detest about the reigning social order: its prosaic longing for security, its unrevolutionary nature, its abhorrence of "transcendence", [and] its anathematization of the vitality and intensity one finds in the "exception" (Schmitt) or "transgression" (Bataille)' (Wolin 1996: 414). For Bataille in particular, the deliberative procedures associated with law were to be replaced with the emotion and excess characteristic of art. Thus Bataille 'seeks to establish the normative basis of social action on an aesthetic foundation' (Wolin 1996: 406). In effect, he aestheticizes the political.

Although it is considerably more polemical in its renunciation of Bataille, Wolin's argument is in many ways predicated on Jürgen Habermas's 'Between Eroticism and General Economy: Georges Bataille' – one of the twelve lectures that make up *The Philosophical Discourse of Modernity*. On Habermas's account, Bataille propagates 'the dream of an aestheticized, poetic politics purified of all institutional and moral elements' (Habermas 1990: 220). In opposition to the subject of modern reason, he fixates on 'explosive moments of fascinated shock, when those categories fall apart that guarantee in everyday life the confident interaction of the subject with himself and with the world' (Habermas 1990: 212). 'Sovereignty', for example, 'is conceived as the other of reason' (Habermas 1990: 228). And yet, Habermas continues, Bataille can only purse this assault on reason while simultaneously relying on the resources of reason. And to that extent, his entire project, and everything that follows from it, is mired in performative contradiction. 'If sovereignty and its source, the sacred, are related to the world of purposive-rational action in an absolutely heterogeneous fashion', Habermas insists:

> if the subject and reason are constituted only by excluding all kinds of sacred power, if the other of reason is more than just the irrational or the unknown – namely, the incommensurable, which cannot be touched by reason except at the cost of an explosion of the rational subject – then there is no possibility of a theory that reaches beyond the horizon of what is accessible to reason and thematizes, let alone analyzes, the interaction of reason with a transcendent source of power. (Habermas 1990: 235-6)

As a result, Habermas concludes, 'Bataille undercuts his own efforts to carry out a radical critique of reason with the tools of theory' (Habermas 1990: 237).

No doubt this challenge – that Bataille seeks to replace rational deliberation with the aesthetic experience or event, but, in order to do so, requires the very reason he wants to destroy – has considerable force, and cannot easily be overlooked. At the same time,

Bataille was by no means unaware of the problem. Indeed, a great deal of his work is taken up with an effort to come to terms with the fact that he must render what remains beyond language, discourse, or knowledge in the form of language, discourse, and knowledge. Moreover, and as I tried to explain towards the end of the last section of this paper, this willingness to negate or erase his own text is one of the things that *distinguishes* Bataille from Schmitt. While Bataille is caught up in a performative contradiction (in that he cannot, at one and the same time, say what he means and mean what he says), Schmitt most assuredly is not. Indeed, by insisting that the sovereign exception operates 'within the framework of the juristic', Schmitt effectively avoids this accusation, and avoids the problem of trying to use discourse to discuss something that exceeds it. In this section of my paper, I would like to suggest that the performative contradiction that Wolin and Habermas detect in Bataille is less a damning criticism of his work than it is a condition – or, perhaps more accurately, a performance – of his ethics. Or, alternatively, it is from this performative contradiction that we, Bataille's readers, might begin to draw an ethics.

A) 'The Insane Silence of the Night'

The central tension in all of Bataille's work is expressed quite clearly in the opening pages of his book *On Nietzsche* – a figure with whom, as Wolin and Habermas correctly note, he not only empathized, but almost completely identified. 'Man's extreme, unconditional yearning was first expressed independently of a moral end or service to God', Bataille writes, 'by Nietzsche':

> This burning with no relation to a dramatically expressed moral obligation is surely paradoxical. It cannot serve as a point of departure for preaching or action. Its consequences are disconcerting. If we cease to make burning the condition of another, further state, one that is distinguished as good, it appears as a pure state, one of empty consumption. Unless related to some enrichment such as the strength and influence of a community (or of a God, a church, a party), this consumption is not even intelligible. The positive value of loss can seemingly be conveyed only in terms of profit. (Bataille 1986b: 47, emphasis in original)

How to understand this 'burning' outside of all 'preaching or action', this 'empty consumption' without reference to a 'further state', or the 'value of loss' outside of all possibility of 'profit' was not only Nietzsche's conundrum, but Bataille's as well. And it had a direct bearing on his practices as a writer. For he could never deny the fact that his own efforts to describe or discuss this 'burning' and this 'consumption' ultimately entailed inscribing them within the register of meaning and sense, thus providing them with an intelligibility, or a kind of return on the investment.

Further examples of Bataille explicitly addressing what Habermas would characterize as the performative contradiction in his work are too numerous to count, and they extend throughout all of the topics he addresses, and all of the genres he employs. For instance, in the preface to 'The History of Eroticism', or the second volume of *The Accursed Share*, Bataille summarizes his argument that all societies require the periodic destruction of excess energy or wealth, and that, while past cultures accomplished this via the sovereign transgression, in the contemporary world, where instrumental rationality dominates, sovereign transgression is replaced by the horrors of mass war. But as soon as Bataille explains this thesis, he feels compelled to acknowledge what he calls the 'paradox' of his 'attitude'. 'The paradox of my attitude requires that I show the absurdity of a system in which each thing *serves*, in which nothing is *sovereign*', he explains. 'I cannot do so without showing that a world in which nothing is sovereign is the most unfavourable one; but,' he continues, 'that is to say in sum that we need sovereign values, hence that it is *useful* to have useless values' (Bataille 1991: 15).

A more poetic articulation of the same paradox pervades *Inner Experience*. Indeed, what Bataille means by 'inner experience' is not the internal world of an individual subject, but an experience that is so singular that it completely eludes the realm of discursive articulation. Here Bataille associates that experience with the spiritual practice of 'supplication', which attempts to mimic 'the exhausting solitude of God':

> Forgetting of everything. Deep descent into the night of existence. Infinite ignorant pleading, to drown oneself in anguish. To slip over the abyss and in the completed darkness experience the horror of it. To tremble, in despair, in the cold of solitude, in the eternal silence of man (foolishness of all sentences, illusory answers for sentences, only the insane silence of the night answers). The word God, to have used it in order to reach the depth of solitude, but to no longer know, hear his voice. To know nothing of him. God final word for meaning that all words will fail further on: to perceive its own eloquence (it is not avoidable), to laugh at it to the point of unknowing stupor (laughter no longer needs to laugh, nor crying to cry, nor sobbing to sob). Further on one's head bursts: man is not contemplation (he only has peace by fleeing); he is supplication, war, anguish, madness. (Bataille 1988: 36-7)

In a manner that is doubtlessly related to negative theology, as well as what, elsewhere, Bataille calls 'atheology', 'God' is the word used to indicate the failure of all words. It marks the limit of discourse in general. It goes without saying that something very different is at stake in Schmitt's invocation of religious language, or 'political theology'. If, for Bataille, theological language is a substitute for something that is always already lost, or that which remains inaccessible to discourse, for Schmitt, it is invariably an allegory for political life, or an indirect way of addressing the exigencies of our collective existence.

As if to punctuate the issue, and to do so from beyond the grave, Bataille himself provides a commentary on the self-negating elements of his writing in a brief 'Autobiographical Note' that was found among his literary remains and published posthumously. The text, which is written in a style that has to be read as ironically rational or controlled, recounts the general arc of Bataille's career, but concludes with the following more personal, though still perfectly chilled, reflections: 'If thought and its expression have become his main area of activity, this has not been without repeated attempts, within the limits of his means, at experiences lacking apparent coherence, but whose very incoherence signifies an effort to comprehend the totality of possibility, or to put it more precisely, to reject, untiringly, any possibility exclusive of others', we read. 'Bataille's aspiration is that of a sovereign existence, free of all limitations of interest'. Here 'the issue is not that of attainment of a goal, but rather of escape from those traps which goals represent'. And then, finally: 'We must elude the task incumbent upon all men, but reserve a share of sovereignty, a share that is irreducible ...

There is work on Bataille's part, but it is an effort to escape, an effort to release toward a freedom that is direct' (Bataille 1986a: 109-110).

There are, no doubt, any number of ways of interpreting these acts of self-negation in Bataille's text, and these efforts to escape the confines of language through the use of language. But by far the most intriguing is the one proposed by Jacques Derrida, in his early essay 'From Restricted to General Economy: A Hegelianism Without Reserve'. Here Derrida suggests that, while none of Bataille's particular attempts to capture the sovereign experience within the confines of language are successful, and while all his attempts to *describe* sovereignty are necessarily inadequate, nevertheless, the manner in which he shifts *between* different attempts to describe sovereignty, developing and relinquishing one network of concepts after another, *performs* or enacts what he means by sovereign, or the sovereign enjoyment of the present without concern for past conditions or future aims. Put crudely, not what Bataille says, but the way he says it, or what Derrida calls the 'form' of his 'writing', is sovereign.

Derrida sets the context for his reading by comparing Hegel's master or lord with Bataille's sovereign. While the former risks death in his battle with the slave, he does so only in the name of a future life, or some promise of the future. The latter, on the other hand, risks an absolute death, without any relation either to the future or to the other. For the same reason, while Hegel's master inhabits the realm of meaning and language, Bataille's sovereign is singular and discrete. But, Derrida notes, this line of thought leads Bataille into a trap of sorts. For it effectively equates 'discourse' with 'the loss of sovereignty' and 'servility' with 'the desire for meaning'. In order to begin to say anything at all, then, or to write about the subject in any manner, Bataille is compelled to 'find a language which remains silent'. He is compelled to accomplish 'the impossible', or 'to say in language – the language of servility – that which is not servile' (Derrida 1978: 262).

According to Derrida, Bataille approaches this 'impossible' task by positing two kinds of language, or '*two* forms of *writing*' (Derrida 1978: 265). The first, which Derrida calls 'minor writing', involves the secondary representation of a more original presence, or what Bataille refers to as the 'mummy' of meaning. The second, which Derrida calls 'major writing', or the 'sovereign form of writing' is not a representation of an original presence, but a chain of substitutions for that which is always already absent (Derrida 1978: 266). Far from imposing a kind of silence or withdrawal, the sovereign form of writing consists of a 'transgressive affirmation' of language. It 'multiplies worlds, precipitates them one against the other, engulfs them too, in an endless and baseless substitution whose only rule is the sovereign affirmation of play outside meaning' (Derrida 1978: 274). And in this manner, even while it speaks, it is effectively 'absolved of every relationship' and 'keeps itself in the night of the secret' (Derrida 1978: 266).

Thus, what Habermas takes to be a performative contradiction, Derrida treats as a performance or an enactment of sovereignty itself. The act of self-negation, or of generating a discourse that is simultaneously erased, signifies, not a failure or error in Bataille's work, but its most essential point. The sovereign experience cannot be represented, or captured within the confines of representational discourse. And for that reason, Bataille is relentlessly shifting between discourses, or languages that have always already missed the mark. But in the act of moving between these discourses, in the act of beginning each time anew, without prior conditions or future promises, Bataille nevertheless manifests sovereignty.

B) The Ethics of Nothing

It remains to be explained what any of this could have to do with ethics. While it might not immediately appear as an ethical project, certainly not from the perspective of traditional ethics, or those which begin with either the rational decisions of a responsible, autonomous subject, or the conventional mores of a delimited moral community, there is nevertheless a fairly clear sense in which Bataille's writing is driven by an imperative, and a privileging of certain experiences over others. In this sense, and as Alan Stoekl notes, Bataille's theory is 'profoundly *ethical*' (Stoekl 2007: 254). But this ethics it not, as Stoekl then goes on to suggest, rooted in Bataille's effort to reassert genuine, sovereign modes of expenditure and waste in the face of modern instrumental reason, which deludes itself into thinking it can do without waste, and in doing so unconsciously mechanizes the process of waste production. As we have already seen, Bataille only advances these claims while resisting or cancelling them out at the same time. Rather, I maintain, for Bataille, it is not the striving for an ideal that is ethical, but the very act of self-negation or self-cancellation – the act, as I have tried to show, that we find repeated over and over again in his writing.

That striving for an ideal cannot be ethical for Bataille seems clear enough. Nothing is more servile, and less sovereign, in his estimation, than allowing future possibility to dictate or dominate the present moment. Even worse, from Bataille's perspective, would be Habermasian discourse ethics, which not only suggests that statements and acts in the present can only be ethical insofar as they are oriented towards the possibility of a future consensus, or an agreement among all interested subjects, but also that such a consensus can never be attained, but is forever altered through the very practical engagements that it regulates, and thus retreats like an eternally unreachable horizon (Habermas 1991). Indeed, it would not be inaccurate to say that, for Bataille, ethics would involve the exact opposite – the rejection or annihilation, not only of all particular interests, but also of all universal norms. Or, we might say, it would have to begin by refusing nearly everything Habermas takes for granted.

Something very close, if not quite identical, to this point is made by Chris Gemerchak, in his article 'Of Goods and Things: Reflections on an Ethical Community'. According to his interpretation, Bataille everywhere resists 'the hegemony of an ethics that adheres to the principle of reason', a principle that invariably 'comes down to the calculations of interest for the good of the individual or a community of individuals and is oriented toward survival in the future rather than life in the present' (Gemerchak 2009: 64). In the place of the calculation of interest and the projection of a future good, Bataille privileges the moments of what he sometimes calls 'intimacy' or 'communication'. Importantly, such things cannot be understood in sanguine liberal terms. They do not involve subjects coming together in pursuit of rational consensus, nor do they involve the absorption of individuals into a kind of oceanic whole. Rather, for Bataille, in intimacy or communication each particular subject is placed, or torn, outside of themselves, not in such a way as to constitute a larger totality, but in such a way as to fragment all totalities, and all efforts to generate an individual or collective unity.

At this point, and like so many others I have discussed in this paper, Gemerchak comes up against the paradox of this approach – the paradox that, as mentioned earlier, Bataille repeatedly admits. It is the paradox of what Gemerchak calls 'the unrelenting work of the dialectical economy, which makes every loss work in the service of a larger community' (Gemerchak 2009: 75). Thus, while the moment of intimacy or communication might involve the complete dissolution of all subjective interests or future purposes, nevertheless, in order to formulate such things as an experience, let alone a discourse, interests and purposes must return. That Bataille himself is compelled, or seems compelled, to write about such things appears, for Gemerchak as for everyone else, to confirm this fact. As a result, and despite the innumerable paths his paper breaks, Gemerchak concludes by suggesting that, inasmuch as there must be one, the maxim of Bataille's ethics would have to read: '*do not give up on your dissatisfaction*' (Gemerchak 2009: 78). Or, to put it differently, do not foreclose the possibility of 'intimacy' and 'communication', or events that challenge the very core of your identity (the very core of identity as such), simply because you know from the outset that, in their wake, some identity must return. Do not say no to risking everything simply because, no matter how much you risk, you know you will get something back.

Here, I think, while Germachak comes very close to Bataille's ethics, and what I am calling 'the ethics of nothing', his proposition needs to be finessed, or modified ever so slightly. For Bataille, I imagine, it would not have been a question of not giving up simply because you know you must fail. Rather, it would have been a question of incorporating your inevitable failure into your act – of affirming, in the moment of intimacy or communication, both the moment, and the failure against which you suspect it is destined to smash. In this way, perhaps, you usurp the power of the future, or deprive it of its authority over the present. You take it up in the present, as part of the present, and of the ecstasy that is the present. This, at any rate, is what Bataille seems to have done in his writing, and in the performances that are his texts. This is how, as Derrida maintains, he transformed his inability to describe sovereignty (or, more accurately, the impossibility of describing sovereignty), and thus his perpetual shifting between descriptions of sovereignty, into an enactment or a performance *of* sovereignty. This is how his text became a living example, rather than a mummified representation, of the sovereign act.

Arendt avec Bataille

In a manner that curiously reflects Bataille's depictions of sovereignty, Hannah Arendt defines action – which she associates with freedom and politics, or with the experience of freedom that is specific to politics – as something that exhausts itself in its expression, and that has no purpose or goal outside of itself. In work, Arendt maintains (again inadvertently reflecting Bataille), humans try to accomplish some task; work is always an instrumental means to an end, and thus subordinate to a future possibility. In action, on the other hand, 'the accomplishment lies in the performance itself, and not in the end product' (Arendt 1993: 154). Action is free precisely because it has, as it were, no future.

As more than a few commentators have pointed out, however, while it might be intellectually compelling, it is not clear how well this conception of action applies to the actual experience or practice of politics. Can we really evacuate politics of all purpose in this fashion? Can we really treat it as a pure performance, devoid of all content save the talent or virtuosity of those involved? Is it not the case that, however minimal or oblique, politics always involves at least some measure of instrumentality, or some effort to advance a project and seek to achieve it? And in that case, would Arendt's abstract definition of action not apply more effectively, not to politics, but to the kinds of experiences that Bataille associates with sovereignty – explosive frenzies of excess (sacrifice, violence, eroticism) and affective, somatic responses (tears, trembling, laughter)?

It is as though Bataille reveals the unspeakable, repressed underside of Arendt's approach to action and politics – and perhaps, by extension, that of the civic republican tradition she represents, and the (as we saw Dylan Riley put it at the beginning of this paper) 'civil society romanticism' (Riley 2010: 2) that often goes along with it. For if we take Arendt's theory of action at its word, in all of its frigid indifference to consequences and effects, then how could we ever distinguish in a rigorous or intellectually satisfying way between, say, the moment when a subject appears before others in word and deed, thereby revealing who as opposed to what they are, and the moment of brutal sacrifice, erotic pleasure, or spontaneous tears? Would the latter not always in some sense haunt the former? And is that perhaps why Arendt is so insistent on confining action to the realm of the political, and separating the political off from all other aspects of the human condition – and most especially, as I note elsewhere, intimacy and love (Barbour 2010)?

Maybe one could imagine composing an argument about Arendt and Bataille modelled on Jacques Lacan's 'Kant avec Sade', where Lacan shows how, inasmuch as it must be purged of all 'hypothetical' concerns, and detached from what Kant called the 'pathological object' (any object that can appeal to one's interests or desires, or any particular good), Kant's 'categorical imperative' constitutes a perfectly cold, abstract machine – one that, because it fixates on an abstract 'Good' that cannot be reduced to any specific, concrete 'good', is ultimately indistinguishable from de Sade's 'philosophy of the bedroom' (Lacan 1986). Similarly, in its complete dissociation from all instrumentality, and all questions of prior conditions or future consequences, Arendt's action cannot be rigorously distinguished from Bataille's sovereignty.

And if that is the case, than perhaps a significantly different approach to the concept of the political – one associated with Lacan's repositioning of ethics in relation to desire (Zupančič 2000) – is required as well. It would, at any rate, be necessary to acknowledge, as Riley impels us to do from a different angle, that civil society is by no means axiomatically democratic, and that there is no simple opposition between the deliberative procedures of civil associations, on the one hand, and the totalitarian fusion of mass politics, on the other; rather, we would have to allow, both endeavour, if also necessarily fail, to foreclose or suppress the experience or the event that Bataille referred to as 'nothingness', and Lacan, the traumatic excesses of the Real.

References

Arendt, H. 1993. 'What is Freedom?'. In *Between Past and Future: Six Exercises in Political Thought*, New York: Penguin, 143–71.

Arendt, H. 2004. *The Origins of Totalitarianism*, New York: Schocken Books.

Barbour, C. 2010. '"Never Seek to Tell Thy Love": Hannah Arendt and the Secret'. In A. Yeatman, et al. (eds), *Action and Appearance: Ethics and the Politics of Writing in Arendt*. London: Continuum.

Bataille, G. 1986a. 'Autobiographical Note'. In *G. Bataille: Writings on Laughter, Sacrifice, Nietzsche, Un-Knowing*. Translated by A. Michelson, Cambridge: The MIT Press.

Bataille, G 1986b. 'On Nietzsche: The Will to Chance'. In *G. Bataille: Writings on Laughter, Sacrifice, Nietzsche, Un-Knowing*. Translated by A. Michelson, Cambridge: The MIT Press.

Bataille, G. 1988. *Inner Experience*. Translated by L. Boldt, Albany: State University of New York Press.

Bataille, G. 1991. *The Accursed Share, Volumes II and III*. Translated by R. Hurley, Cambridge: The MIT Press.

de Tocqueville, Alexis 2003. *Democracy in America*. Translated by G. Bevan. London: Penguin.

Derrida, J. 1978. 'From Restricted to General Economy: A Hegelianism Without Reserve'. In *Writing and Difference*. Translated by A. Bass, Chicago: University of Chicago Press.

Gemerchak, C. 2009. 'Of Goods and Things: Reflections on an Ethics of Community'. In A. J. Mitchell et al. (eds), *The Obsessions of Georges Bataille: Community and Communication,*. Albany: SUNY Press.

Geroulanos, S. 2010. *An Atheism that is not Humanist Emerges in French Thought*, Stanford: Stanford University Press.

Habermas, J. 1990. 'Between Eroticism and General Economics: Georges Bataille'. In *The Philosophical Discourse of Modernity: Twelve Lectures*. Translated by F. Lawrence, Cambridge: The MIT Press.

Habermas, J. 1991. *Moral Consciousness and Communicative Action*. Translated by C. Lenhardt and Shierry Weber Nicholsen, Cambridge: The MIT Press.

Jay, M. 1993. 'The Reassertion of Sovereignty in a Time of Crisis: Carl Schmitt and Georges Bataille'. In *Force Fields: Between Intellectual History and Cultural Critique*, New York: Routledge.

Lacan, J. 1986. 'Kant with Sade'. Translated by J. Swenson, *October*, 51: 55-75.

Levi, N. 2007. 'Carl Schmitt and the Question of the Aesthetic'. *New German Critique*, 34 2.: 27-43.

Nancy, J. 1991. 'Exscription'. Translated by K. Lydon. *Yale French Studies*, 79, 47-65.

Riley, D. 2010. *The Civic Foundations of Fascism in Europe: Italy, Spain, and Romania, 1870-1945*, Baltimore: The Johns Hopkins University.

Schmitt, C. 2005. *Political Theology: Four Chapters on the Concept of Sovereignty*. Translated by G. Schwab, Chicago: University of Chicago Press.

Stoekl, A. 2007. 'Excess and Depletion: Bataille's Surprisingly Ethical Model of Expenditure'. In *Reading Bataille Now*, S. Winnubst, (eds) Bloomington: Indiana University Press.

Wolin, R. 1996. 'Left Fascism: Georges Bataille and the German Ideology'. *Constellations*, 2:3, 397-428.

Wolin, R. 2004. *The Seduction of Unreason: The Intellectual Romance with Fascism from Nietzsche to Postmodernism*, Princeton: Princeton University Press.

Zupančič, A. 2000. *Ethics of the Real: Kant, Lacan*, London: Verso.

The Ends of Stasis: Spinoza as a Reader of Agamben

Dimitris Vardoulakis

Abstract *Agamben contends that 'There is ... no such thing as a stasiology, a theory of stasis or civil war' in the western understanding of sovereignty. His own vision of a politics beyond biopolitics explicitly culminates in the end of stasis. How can we understand Agamben's political theology by investigating his use of stasis? Stasis is particularly suited to an inquiry into political theology. It is linked to politics, since its primary meaning is political change, revolution, or civil war, as well as to the theological, since it denotes immobility or immutability, which were attributes of God. Stasis, then, presents the simultaneous presence and absence that exemplifies the unassimilable relation of the sacred and the secular in political theology. The question is: Does Agamben remain true to this unassimilable relation? Or does he betray it the moment he calls for an end to biopolitics? Agamben's reading of Spinoza will provide useful clues in answering these questions.*

I. On stasis

In a paper titled 'The State of Exception', Agamben contends that 'There is ... no such thing as a stasiology, a theory of stasis or civil war' in the western understanding of sovereignty (Agamben 2005a: 284–85).[1] His own vision of a politics beyond biopolitics explicitly culminates in the end of stasis:

> Only a politics that will have learned to take the fundamental biopolitical fracture of the West into account will be able ... to put an end to the civil war that divides the peoples and the cities of the earth. (Agamben 1998: 180)[2]

Agamben first calls for the inclusion of stasis in the determination of the political only so that stasis is excluded from politics. This strategy is revealing, because Agamben's definition of the sovereign rests precisely on the logic of inclusory exclusion. Eva Geulen has called this 'the logic of the exception' but it can equally be called the 'logic of the sovereign' or even the 'logic of

---

[1] This paragraph and its call for a stasiology can be read as a summary of Agamben's argument in the second sequel to the *Homo Sacer* project, *State of Exception* (Agamben 2005b).

[2] The same statement can also be found in Agamben 2000: 35.

politics' (Geulen 2005: 73–82). The present paper will examine Agamben's theory of sovereignty by comparing his call for an end to stasis with his logic of inclusory exclusion.

The word 'stasis' (στάσις) means, on the one hand, immobility, stability, status quo; and, on the other, it means mobility, upheaval, revolution.[3] Both these contradictory meanings of stasis underlie political discourse. Stasis is the root of the word for the 'state' in English – as well as the equivalent words in all languages which derive the name for the body politic from Latin, such as 'Staat' in German. Thomas Hobbes, however, rendered stasis as 'sedition' in his translation of Thucydides' *Histories*.[4] The same word, then, represents both the sovereign power and the power of revolt or even civil war. Stasis establishes the constellation of relations of the impossible possibility of the political (see Vardoulakis 2009).

As soon as the political is tied to the 'impossible possibility' of a word, the question inevitably arises of a politics of reading. The way words are read is symptomatic of the status of the theoretical construction of the political. In addition, as Bauman observes, 'resistance to definition sets the limit to sovereignty' (Bauman 1990: 166). This politics of reading arises from within stasis itself, because stasis has a third meaning, disease or infection. Disease will allow for the other two – mobility and immobility, the status quo and the revolution – to come in a productive relation. As will be shown, the way the third meaning of stasis is used within a discourse about politics determines of how sovereignty as well as revolution is understood. I will argue that disease points to a nothing at the core of sovereignty, in the sense that there is something unconditional which organises political discourse.

The admonition to 'put an end to the civil war that divides the peoples and the cities of the earth' is, then, not a simple statement against civil war. Rather, it is indicative of the operation of stasis in Agamben's political philosophy. The different meanings of stasis enact the juncture between civil war and the sovereign – 'the proximity between civil war and the state of exception' in Agamben's formulation. For this reason, the way the three meanings of stasis – mobility, immobility, and disease – are related in a particular discourse is simultaneously the articulation of that discourse's notion of the sovereign. Agamben's logic of inclusory exclusion, then, is produced by stasis's dual aspect: being created, on the one hand, through the specific articulation of its elements, while being creative, on the other, of the sovereign.

The sovereign in Agamben arises out of passivity, which is extrapolated in terms of disease – that is, in terms of one of stasis's meanings. Passivity or disease as the foundation of sovereignty results in a rupture between the

---

[3] See the entry for stasis in Liddell and Scott (1973). The most significant book on stasis is Nicole Loraux's *The Divided City* (2006). The most thorough philological study on the use of stasis in classical Greek sources is Hans-Joachim Gehrke, *Stasis* (1985); see also Kostas Kalimtzis, *Aristotle on Political Enmity and Disease* (2000).

[4] This translation, published in 1629, was Hobbes' first significant work.

political and law.[5] Agamben articulates this rupture as the separation of ethics from politics. Agamben's references to Spinoza will show the effect the politics of reading has on the political. Spinoza, the philosopher of joy, is incorporated in Agamben's opposing project that privileges disease. Thus the Spinozan corpus rehearses the logic of inclusion followed by exclusion that characterises Agamben's stasiology. Therefore, Spinoza's corpus allows for a critical reading of Agamben. Spinoza becomes a reader of Agamben in the sense that a critique of Agamben will arise out of his reading of Spinoza. There is no secured outside – no separate criteria – which affords a critique of Agamben. This is important because Agamben posits such an outside in order to legitimate both his notion of the political and his practice of reading.

I will first show how the three meanings of stasis organise Agamben's conception of the political. I will then demonstrate how Agamben's references to Spinoza are crucial in allowing for a theoretical perspective on stasis. The way this is done, I will argue, shows that singularity is absent from Agamben's notion of the political. At that point I will explain how the absence of singularity is interconnected with Agamben's practice of reading, leading to a politics of reading. I will conclude by indicating how stasis can allow for a different construal of sovereignty from the one espoused by Agamben.

II. Passive politics

The arrangement of the three different meanings of stasis – mobility, immobility, and disease – is indicative of the construal of the sovereign in Agamben. The distinctive feature of Agamben's political philosophy is the privileging of passivity as disease. The paradigm of passivity for Agamben is the *Muselmann*. That was the name given to the most abject inmates in the Nazi concentration camps described by Primo Levi and others. The *Muselmann* is 'a being from whom humiliation, horror, and fear has so taken away all consciousness and all personality as to make him absolutely apathetic' (Agamben 1998: 185). Absolute apathy is disease.

Agamben's term 'biopolitics' signifies a double basis of the political: the exclusion of the biological or 'bare life' – the exclusion of passivity – from the public sphere, only for it to be re-introduced by sovereign power.[6] The separation of bare life from public life as 'the production of a biopolitical body is the original activity of sovereign power' (Agamben 1998: 6). The *sine qua non* of this logic of politics is a diseased body thoroughly separated from politics.

---

[5] See Agamben 1998: 1–3, and *passim*. Agamben often refers to bare life as *zoe* and to political life as *bios*, and he traces their separation back to Aristotle. It is curious – to the point of being spurious – to suppose such a distinction in Aristotle. The most cursory reading of either the *Nicomachean Ethics* or the *Politics* will show that Aristotle's favourite expression to refer to the aim of politics is *to eu zen*, the happy life, of the citizen. For example, in *Politics* 1280b Aristotle says: 'τέλος μὲν οὖν πόλεως τὸ εὖ ζῆν' [the aim of the polis is the happy life].

[6] The term 'biopolitics' is borrowed from Foucault. For a discussion of Agamben's curious reading of Foucault's last chapter of the first volume of *The History of Sexuality* see Fitzpatrick (2001: 13–14). Fitzpatrick also questions Agamben's reading of the term *homo sacer* in Roman law.

The *Muselmann*'s apathy offers, according to Agamben, an alternative politics. As an 'absolutely apathetic' body, the *Muselmann* 'no longer belongs to the world of men in any way. Mute and absolutely alone, he passes into another world' (Agamben 1998: 185). The disease of the *Muselmann* places him in a realm of the outside. Agamben defines this 'other world' as a space of 'an absolute indistinction of fact and law, of life and juridical order, of nature and politics' (Agamben 1998: 185). This enacts the traditional sovereign gesture of violence separating passion and action, the animal and the human; but it also reconfigures human agency as an auto-affection, leading to a new definition of the human: '[Fundamental passivity] undergoes and suffers its own being ... Every human power is *adynamia*' (Agamben 1999b: 182). Passivity indicates the negativity pervading Agamben's redefinition of the human.

Through fundamental passivity Agamben's new subject internalises the founding sovereign violence and hence coincides with the sovereign. Agamben's notion of sovereignty is located at the point where passivity and activity enter a zone of indistinction. This zone exhibits the internalised conflict – or stasis as immobility – between the *Muselmann* and the sovereign. In Agamben's challenging formulation, 'in the person of the Führer, bare life passes immediately into law, just as in the person of the camp inhabitant (or neomort) [i.e., the *Muselmann*] law becomes indistinguishable from biological life' (Agamben 1998: 187). In the zone of indistinction crystallises an immobility or stand off between the passive – bare life, the purely biological, the diseased body – and the sovereign. The two become indistinguishable, no effective difference remains between the *Muselmann* and the Führer.

A determination of the law is adjacent to the determination of the sovereign. Agamben insists on a rupture between passivity and law.[7] The sovereign's violence founding the political is grounded on disease or passivity. But disease is ungrounded. The 'naked life' of the diseased is not reducible to a citizen's body framed by statute. Hence an ethics does not coincide with rules and norms – an ethics is incommensurable with politics.[8] This move is crucial in understanding Agamben's stasiology, since is refers to mobility or upheaval – the third element of stasis. Politics and law are indistinct from the point of view of the body's passivity and the sovereign's violence.[9] But simultaneously, from the perspective of mobility, ethics and law are incommensurate. From this insurmountable gap, Agamben will infer that it is possible to separate ethics from politics. This separation is indispensable in Agamben's stasiology, envisioning a politics beyond biopolitics which will 'put an end to the civil war that divides the peoples and cities of the

---

[7] This separation is presented in various ways in Agamben's works. For instance, it is presented as the separation between constituent and constituted power in Agamben 1998: 43–4, referring to Negri. The same separation between constituent and constituted power is argued for in Agamben (2005b) with recourse to Carl Schmitt (Agamben 2005b: 33, 36, 50, 54)

[8] Bernstein (2004) has critiqued this position.

[9] Erik Vogt correctly notes that, for Agamben, 'boundaries between politics and law are equally indistinguishable, since sovereignty and the sovereign exception are marked too by an inclusive exclusion' (2005: 78).

earth'. For Agamben, the end, or aim, of stasis is the end, or cessation, of the correlation between ethics and politics. The end, in both senses of the word, is built upon the apathetic body of the *Muselmann* stranded in a zone of indistinction.

III. Absolute immanence, or the passion for theory

There is no theory without recourse to a notion of generality or universality. Founding sovereignty on passivity to the exclusion of the divine entails that a generalised theory becomes problematic. To counteract this, Agamben resorts to the concept of absolute immanence. Absolute immanence is linked to stasiology because 'the extreme situation's lesson is that of absolute immanence'. Agamben defines absolute immanence as a state 'of "everything being in everything"' (Agamben 2002: 50). In his paper titled 'Absolute Immanence', Agamben (1999a) argues that Spinoza fails to present the proper relation between the three elements of stasis.[10] Through this reading, Agamben can forge his own claim to a theory of the political beyond biopolitics.

Absolute immanence is nuanced with recourse to Spinoza's notion of the immanent cause: 'through Spinoza's idea of an immanent cause in which agent and patient coincide, Being is freed from the risk of inertia and immobility' (Agamben 1999a: 226). The coincidence of action and passion is auto-affection, which according to Agamben designates Spinoza's immanent cause. The whole argument depends upon the extrapolation of immanent causality. The example of a self-reflexive verb, *pasearse*, from Spinoza's *Hebrew Grammar*, is taken as the 'equivalent for an immanent cause' in the sense that in it 'agent and patient enter a threshold of absolute indistinction' (Agamben 1999a: 234). Thus, absolute immanence enters a zone of indistinction. Consequently, absolute immanence is 'a potentiality without action' thereby 'being instead the matrix of infinite desubjectification' (Agamben 1999a: 232–33). Agamben contends that this is what Spinoza calls beatitude or blessed life. In the end, Agamben's verdict is that beatitude 'once again produce[s] transcendence', because 'today, blessed life lies on the same terrain as the biopolitical body of the West' (Agamben 1999a: 238–39).[11] In Spinoza, there is no separation between ethics and politics.

Agamben argues that to escape the 'biopolitical body of the West', the experience of desubjectification must be radicalised. For this to be accomplished, a sovereign space must be created in which the subject overcomes the conjunction of the pleasurable and the political. The subject must first enter the zone of indistinction. Agamben presents Spinoza as a precursor, in the sense that the immanent cause is described as creating such a zone. However,

---

[10] The paper 'Absolute Immanence' is also an interpretation of Deleuze (1997), however, this interpretation will not be discussed here. Agamben also mentions Spinoza elsewhere in his work, but in many cases only as passing references (for example Agamben 1993: 18–19 and 90–91) that will not then be discussed here. Nor will chapter 7 of Agamben 1999b be discussed here, since it is really about Elsa Morante's reading of Spinoza and not Spinoza's work itself at all.

[11] The translation 'biological body' has been amended to 'biopolitical body', since the original text in Italian says 'il corpo biopolitico' (Agamben 1996: 57).

Spinoza is said to have not gone far enough. The subject must be placed *outside* the terrain of biopolitics and blessed life in order to overcome biopolitics. In other words, what is missing in Spinoza is the element of the diseased body – the body of the apathetic *Muselmann*. Only the diseased body can lead to a separation of ethics and politics that will show the end of stasis.

However, Spinoza is re-incorporated in Agamben's project. Rejecting Spinoza's presentation of the immanent cause as a possible description of God, while re-interpreting the immanent cause in terms of desubjectification, enables Agamben to present a unified subject that underwrites his own theory of a politics beyond biopolitics.

Agamben gives his argument a formality through decontextualisation. Such decontextualisation, achieved through the reference to Spinoza's *Hebrew Grammar*, makes generality possible. The desubjectified self is now described as unitary. The witness as a 'unitary center' witnesses only 'an irreducible negativity', that is, pure passivity or disease (see Agamben 2002: 86). What was missing in Spinoza is the grounding of auto-affection of a purely passive body – an apathetic body whose sensations are internalised. Spinoza glimpsed at such a conception in his *Grammar* but did not fully develop it. This auto-affective state fully *in*-corporates biopolitics. This 'unitary centre' of subjectivity is in a zone of indistinction outside the political beyond rules and norms – in other words, designating stasis's mobility. Even though such disease is ruptured from the political, its inclusion in the zone of indistinction or immobility constitutes the ground of the political. This zone is, for Agamben, produced by the passive, apathetic, diseased body.

Spinoza is presented as Agamben's forerunner in the sense that he grasped biopolitics but was criticised because he did not go far enough.[12] Spinoza is included within Agamben's ambit only in order to be excluded. This reverberation of the biopolitical sovereign logic of inclusion *cum* exclusion elevates Spinoza to a figure of Agambian biopolitics. This is carried out in terms denoting stasis's constellation of meanings. Spinoza's position, Agamben contends, is infected by the lack of disease. Spinoza, especially in his *Grammar*, sets up the conditions to make disease central for the political but he does not include disease in his corpus. Thus Agamben re-enacts on the site of citing Spinoza's construal of embodiment – on Spinoza's body – the gesture *par excellence* of biopolitics. Agamben's stasiological practice of reading Spinoza, therefore, has to do with the body. Spinoza's incorporation ineluctably poses the question: how does Agamben's critique admit of embodiment in his politics?

IV. Ineffective subjectivity

The answer is that Agamben needs no notion of embodiment for a politics beyond biopolitics. Agamben's stasiology is predicated upon the absence of singularity. This can only be maintained by eliminating effectivity from a theorisation of the political.

---

[12] As Adam Thurschwell (2005) has shown, Agamben uses a similar appropriation of Derrida.

The loss of singularity due to the abstraction of the body can be gleaned from the following statement: 'If … the essence of the camp consists in the materialization of the state of exception, and in the subsequent creation of a space in which bare life and juridical order enter into a threshold of indistinction, then we must admit that we find ourselves in the presence of a camp *every time* such a structure is created, *independent of the kinds of crime that are committed there*' (Agamben 1998: 174). Agamben's ontology is premised on the general or the 'every time', not on effective singularity.[13] It will be recalled that Agamben defines the *Muselmann* as not belonging 'to the world of men' but being instead 'mute and absolutely alone' (Agamben 1998: 185). The sovereign subject resulting from apathy has literally taken everything in: passivity leads to impunity. At this place, instead of the plurality of men, instead of the singularity of each individual case, Agamben's gaze is fastened onto an immaterial image he calls 'the *Muselmann*'.[14] The definite article next to an abstracted substantive means that the syntagm 'the Muselmann' functions as an absolute immanence, a subject of 'everything being in everything' (Agamben 2002: 50). This is a subject *for, on, in, through*, and *by* – but *never with* – with which Agamben's politics of total immanence engages for the future cessation of all civil wars.[15] This totalised subjectivity becomes the ground of the political, despite being placed outside singularity. This is a solitary subject, stranded in its own other-worldly zone of indistinction. From this perspective, Agamben's call for an end to stasis denotes a subject standing alone, a subject that cannot effect any conflict outside itself. Everyone is in everyone, all distinctions – including that of the other and the friend – completely evaporate.[16]

Agamben critiques Spinoza on the grounds that he did not allow for separation. But Agamben's own critique – tautologically – presupposes separation and is separated from Spinoza's discourse. What is the effect of this presupposed mutual support between Agamben's critique and his theory of sovereignty? In other words, how does Agamben's ontology relate to his practice of reading? It would be too easy to point out that the loss of singularity and the effect is contrary to the whole of Spinoza's philosophical project, since both in politics and metaphysics it is crucial how the effects express the

---

[13] Andreas Kalyvas has also taken Agamben's conception of temporality to task, writing: '*Homo Sacer* returns to a representation of time – the tie of the sovereign – as uniform, one-directional, and rectilinear' (2005: 111). This general position on time, Kalyvas argues, becomes the ground for Agamben's historical extrapolation of sovereignty: 'Sovereign biopolitics … has uninterruptedly accompanied the ancients and the moderns alike, remaining unaffected by critical events' (2005: 111). The upshot of this understanding of sovereignty as a perennial quality is a loss of singularity: 'By disregarding the distinct aspects of political power, politics is relegated to a single, pejorative version of sovereign power and state authority' (Kalyvas 2005: 115).

[14] Philippe Mesnard (2004) objects precisely to this structure of negative theology in Agamben's discussion of the *Muselmann*.

[15] In Catherine Mills' words: 'What Agamben fails to take into account, though, is that the taking place of enunciation can itself be seen as always a matter of 'being-with' others' (2005: 211).

[16] This corresponds to what Carl Schmitt (1998) calls political romanticism.

cause (see, for instance, Deleuze 1992; Negri 2002; Balibar 1998). What is more interesting is how Agamben's ontology is intimately linked with a practice of reading. Here, stasis brings together critique and the political.

V. The sovereign reader

Agamben concentrates on Spinoza's *Hebrew Grammar*. As grammatical examples, the examples from the *Hebrew Grammar* are syntagms uttered by nobody in no place. They are linguistic forms placed outside the effects and use of language. As Nicholas Chare puts it, 'For Agamben language is an out-of-body experience' (2006: 59). Agamben's reading of Spinoza through grammar is, then, violently decontextualised – and, yet, because of that, all the more symptomatic of Agamben's paradigm of reading. Crucially, Agamben rehearses in the theory of the grammatical example the theory of sovereign constitution through the exception: 'exception and example are correlative concepts that are ultimately indistinguishable and that come into play every time the sense of belonging and commonality of individuals is to be defined' (Agamben 1998: 22; see also Agamben 2005b: 36–37). The sovereign logic of inclusory exclusion, Agamben contends, is the same in grammar and in politics. Thus Agamben's references to Spinoza's *Hebrew Grammar* can be taken as the exemplary example of the theory of sovereignty based on disease.

The crucial point in Agamben's readings from the *Hebrew Grammar* is the correlation between self-reflexivity and the immanent cause. Agamben argues that in the *Hebrew Grammar*, 'the philosopher explains the meaning of the reflexive active verb as an expression of an immanent cause, that is, of an action in which agent and patient are one and the same person'. Agamben cites from Chapter 20 of the *Hebrew Grammar* the example of a verb in the middle voice, *pasearse*, which is translated as 'to walk-oneself' (Agamben 1999a: 234). Therefore, Agamben contends, Spinoza asserts a coincidence between immanent causality and the auto-affection of subjectivity – its passivity *cum* activity that characterises the zone of indistinction. This claim is problematic. Immanent causality as such is not the same as either the middle voice, or the activity and passivity of an agent or the subject of a sentence.[17] Thus, Agamben's claim must be that Spinoza *specifically* makes this point. However, Chapter 20 nowhere makes such a contention. Spinoza here merely describes the middle voice in grammatical terms – 'the accusative is not

---

[17] It does not follow from the distinction between nominative (the subject) and accusative (the object) that there is a positing of human agency independent of its environment. As Jacques Derrida put it, 'that which lets itself be designated *différance* is neither simply active nor simply passive, announcing or rather recalling something like the middle voice, saying an operation that is not an operation, an operation that cannot be conceived either as a passion or as the action of an agent or patient, neither on the basis of nor moving toward any of these *terms*' (1984: 9). This erasure of agency and the ensuing sense of community is the lynchpin of John Llewelyn's discussion of the middle voice in the most interesting recent book on the topic (Llewelyn 1991).

different from the nominative' – making no mention whatsoever of immanent causality.[18]

Immanent causality in Spinoza's writings clearly has nothing to do with human agency or subjectivity. Perhaps the most important discussion of the immanent cause is Proposition 18 from Part I of the *Ethics*. 'God', says Spinoza, 'is the immanent ... cause of all things'.[19] This Proposition immediately follows a significant Scholium in which Spinoza argues against anthropomorphism, or the attribution of intellect and will to God. In other words, the notion of the immanent cause is conceived in such a way as to be reducible neither to an action, nor to a passion, nor to a combination of the two. Agamben's concept of subjective auto-affection has nothing to do with Spinoza's immanent causality.[20]

A fundamentally passive subject does not exist in a world in which effect can be eliminated. To the question 'who can be such a subject?', the answer can only be Agamben himself as the reader of Spinoza. Agamben, as the 'unitary centre' of the reading self, reads Spinoza as his own auto-affection. Immanent causality loses any real references to particular texts by Spinoza. They are transported to the zone of reading whose sovereign is Agamben himself. The *effect* of this reading – because, *pace* Agamben, effectivity cannot be neutralised – is a liberal *free-for-all* disposition. What matters is not the text, but the examples excised from the text. Agamben, in a passage cited earlier, contended that the logic of inclusory exclusion can generalise his theory of

---

[18] Even though Spinoza does use the words 'immanent cause' in Chapter 12 of the *Hebrew Grammar*, whence Agamben derives a second example, Spinoza is nevertheless not making any philosophical claim about immanent causality here but merely trying to explain the middle voice. In fact, Agamben's translation of the Latin is rather misleading. In Latin it is clear throughout Chapter 12 that Spinoza is positioning the reflexive between the active and the passive mood (*ad agentem* and *ad patientem*). Thus, when Spinoza writes 'Ideoque necesse fuit Infinitivorum speciem excogitare, quae actionem exprimeret ad agentem, sive causam immanentem relatam' (Spinoza 1924, I: 342), this is accurately translated by Maurice J. Bloom as: 'Therefore it was necessary to devise another form of infinitive which would express an action related to the active mood or to the imminent cause' (Spinoza 2002: 629). Spinoza's point is grammatical, not philosophical, and it is a point about the relation between the different moods. Thus, Agamben's translation of the subordinate clause is rather surprising: 'which expresses an action referred to an agent as immanent cause' ['*che esprimesse l'azione riferita all'agente come causa immanente*'] (Agamben 1999b: 235; 1996: 52). Agamben's translation erroneously suggests that Spinoza is talking here about an individual which acts as (*come*) an immanent cause. Spinoza's point, however, is much more uncontroversial: in the active voice, the subject itself is the cause of the action. There is nothing in the text of Chapter 12 to suggest that Spinoza is advancing a theory of action, or of agency, or of individuation.

[19] God as 'causa immanens' is one of the important aspects of Part I of the *Ethics*. The definition of Proposition 18 is already implicit from at least Proposition 15, although the whole of the preceding of Part I can be seen as leading up to Proposition 18. On God and causality – including God as an immanent cause – see also *Short Treatise*, Part I, Chapters 2 and 3, as well as the final chapter of the *Short Treatise*. For the sources of Spinoza's understanding of divine causality, see volume 1 of Wolfson (1969).

sovereignty: 'we find ourselves in the presence of a camp every time such a structure is created, independent of the kinds of crime that are committed there' (Agamben 1998: 174). Following this his theory of reading as an effect of the example must follow a strictly symmetrical logic: 'we find ourselves in the presence of such a grammatical structure as the one derived from the *Hebrew Grammar* every time we read, independent of the text, and independent of the bodies who have written those texts in a particular place and time'. The sovereign as a reading or as a political entity is produced by the same logic. The body – as singular body *and* as body of work – has been internalised within the sovereign. That body – Spinoza's body – thus becomes the exemplary body for the sovereign reader: Agamben himself.

VI. The reader of stasis

Homo Sacer concludes with a series of grand statements. The overcoming of biopolitics is part of the 'destiny of the West', says Agamben, followed by the apocalyptic warning that otherwise the West is facing an 'unprecedented biopolitical catastrophe'. These statements culminate in the call for an end to stasis – to 'put an end to the civil war that divides the peoples and the cities of the earth'. Such statements cannot hide the invidious and eroding circularity of a sovereign's vision of the future, both material and immaterial, both here and there, one moment triumphal, the next stern but always prophetic. The diseased body – the first element of stasis in Agamben's construal – has founded a politics that elects a sovereign who destines his own self-incurred destiny.

The same movement has been shown to take place in a process of reading that equates the grammatical example and the exception. The reading subject assumes a sovereign position of absolute impunity – a poetico-political licence for an endless internalisation of discourse. The end of stasis is also the end of critique as an activity that allows for a text to be effective.

Stasis, however, cannot be neutralised. The pronouncement of its end exhibits the ends symptomatic of a totalising – that is, sovereign – discourse. These symptoms have appeared through the mediation of Spinoza's corpus. Spinoza is a reader of Agamben because Agamben's critique of Spinoza's lack of a diseased body to found the political gives rise precisely to the means of

---

[20] Agamben also offers a similarly curious reading of beatitude. With reference to *Ethics*, Part III, Proposition 51, Agamben argues that beatitude is the same as the immanent cause (see for instance Agamben 1999a: 237). But towards the end of Part III of the *Ethics*, Spinoza has already defined affectivity and is well on the way to providing a typology of emotions. In the end of the Scholium to Proposition 51, cited by Agamben, Spinoza defines passions which are conceived by the mind as being self-caused. The two passions are repentance (*paenitentia*) and self-contentment (*acquiescentia in se ipso*, which Agamben translates as 'being at rest in oneself'). The former gives the impression that the self causes its own pain, while the latter its own pleasure. There is no direct or indirect reference to beatitude, and the idea of beatitude – a joyful union with God – is entirely out of place at this point of the *Ethics*. According to *Ethics* IV, Propositions 54–57, repentance and self-satisfaction belong to the first kind of knowledge because they are self-caused, and not to the third kind of knowledge and to beatitude, whose cause of pleasure is the idea of God.

unravelling Agamben's own political discourse about the end to stasis. The effect and singularity can be retained – Spinoza can be a reader of Agamben – only if there is no constitutive separation within or through stasis.

To resist such a separation is to retain responsibility for the political and for reading. Spinoza as a reader of Agamben points to responsibility, first of all, by pointing to an unconditional remainder in reading practice. There is no sovereign reader who is immune from the traces left by his own reading practice. To read 'disease' is to effect one's own reading with that disease. There is no position from which a comfortable separation of disease from the norms and rules of a community can offer a secure foundation. But this is already to suggest that stasis allows for a positive articulation of reading practice: Spinoza the reader of Agamben suggests that *critique* must always be a response to the text read. This critical response *includes* rules and norms, even though it does not coincide with them. The fact that disease remains unconditional entails that disease is a principle of reading, a principle of response to the text, which puts into question every effort to transform it into a foundation. Disease, in this set up, negates presence. It functions as the nothing wherein presence cannot be secured.

The political can also be articulated positively as the praxis of responsibility. A responsible politics incorporates the unconditional. It incorporates disease as the element which – *pace* Agamben – confounds all foundations. To be responsible is precisely to remain vigilant about any discourse that seeks to find a foundation. A responsible politics is above all a politics that eschews the violent act of separation instituting the sovereign. Stasis solicits a politics of friendship. This is a politics that views as central the intertwining of the ethical and the political. Both ethics and politics refer to praxis, to acts of particularity. But such practice is 'infected' with singularity, irreducible to all-encompassing abstractions. Stasis, then, does not lead to a nothing as pure absence either. Rather, stasis becomes the responsibility to infinitely respond in such a way as to retain the singularity of the response.

References

Agamben, G. 1993. *The Coming Community*. Translated by M. Hardt. Minneapolis, MN: University of Minnesota Press.

Agamben, G. 1996. 'L'immanenza assoluta'. *aut aut* 276, 39–57.

Agamben, G. 1998. *Homo Sacer: Sovereign Power and Bare Life*. Translated by D. Heller-Roazen. Stanford, CA: Stanford University Press.

Agamben, G. 1999a. 'Absolute Immanence'. In D. Heller-Roazen (ed), *Potentialities: Collected Essays in Philosophy*. Translated by D. Heller-Roazen. Stanford, CA: Stanford University Press, 220–39.

Agamben, G. 1999b. *The End of the Poem: Studies in Poetics*. Translated by D. Heller-Roazen. Stanford, CA: Stanford University Press.

Agamben, G. 2000. *Means Without End: Notes on Politics*. Translated by V. Binnetti and C. Casarino. Minneapolis, MN: University of Minnesota Press.

Agamben, G. 2002. *Remnants of Auschwitz: The Witness and the Archive*. Translated by D. Heller-Roazen. New York: Zone Books.

Agamben, G. 2005a. 'The State of Exception'. Translated by G. Agamben and K. Attell. In A. Norris (ed), *Politics, Metaphysics, and Death: Essays on Giorgio Agamben's 'Homo Sacer'*. Durham, NC: Duke University Press, 284–98.

Agamben, G. 2005b. *State of Exception*. Translated by K. Attell. Chicago, IL: University of Chicago Press.

Balibar, É. 1998. *Spinoza and Politics*. Translated by P. Snowdon. London: Verso.

Bauman, Z. 1990. 'Modernity and Ambivalence'. *Theory, Culture & Society* 7, 143–69.

Bernstein, J. M. 2004. 'Bare Life, Bearing Witness: Auschwitz and the Pornography of Horror'. *Parallax* 10:1, 2–16.

Chare, N. 2006. 'The Gap in the Context: Giorgio Agamben's *Remnants of Auschwitz*'. *Cultural Critique* 64, 40–68.

Deleuze, G. 1992. *Expressionism in Philosophy: Spinoza*. Translated by M. Joughin. New York: Zone Books.

Deleuze, G. 1997. 'Immanence: A Life…'. Translated by N. Millett. *Theory, Culture and Society* 14:2, 3–7.

Derrida, J. 1984. 'Différance'. In *Margins of Philosophy*. Translated by A. Bass. Chicago, IL: University of Chicago Press, 1–28.

Fitzpatrick, P. 2001. 'Bare Sovereignty: *Homo Sacer* and the Insistence of the Law'. *Theory and Event* 5.2. Available online: http://muse.jhu.edu/ (accessed 12 January 2010).

Gehrke, H.-J. 1985. *Stasis: Untersuchungen zu den inneren Kriegen in den griechischen Staaten des 5. und 4. Jahrhunderts v. Chr.*. Munich: Beck.

Geulen, E. 2005. *Giorgio Agamben zur Einführung*. Hamburg: Junius.

Kalimtzis, K. 2000. *Aristotle on Political Enmity and Disease: An Inquiry into Stasis*. New York: SUNY Press.

Kalyvas, A. 2005. 'The Sovereign Weaver: Beyond the Camp'. In A. Norris (ed), *Politics, Metaphysics, and Death: Essays on Giorgio Agamben's 'Homo Sacer'*. Durham, NC: Duke University Press, 107–34.

Liddell, H. G. and Scott, R. 1973. *A Greek-English Lexicon*. Revised by H. Stuart Jones. London: Oxford University Press.

Llewelyn, J. 1991. *The Middle Voice of Ecological Conscience: A Chiasmic Reading of Responsibility in the Neighborhood of Levinas, Heidegger and Others*. New York: St. Martin's Press.

Loraux, N. 2006. *The Divided City: On Memory and Forgetting in Ancient Athens*. Translated by C. Pache and F. Fort. New York: Zone Books.

Mesnard, P. 2004. 'The Political Philosophy of Giorgio Agamben: A Critical Evaluation'. Translated by C. Guiat. *Totalitarian Movements and Political Religions* 5:1, 139–57.

Mills, C. 2005. 'Linguistic Survival and Ethicality: Biopolitics, Subjectification, and Testimony in Remnants of Auschwitz'. In A. Norris (ed), *Politics, Metaphysics, and Death: Essays on Giorgio Agamben's 'Homo Sacer'*. Durham, NC: Duke University Press, 198–221.

Negri, A. 2002. *The Savage Anomaly: The Power of Spinoza's Metaphysics and Politics*. Translated by M. Hardt. Minneapolis, MN: University of Minnesota Press.

Schmitt, C. 1998 [1919]. *Politische Romantik*. Berlin: Duncker & Humblot.

Spinoza, B. 1924. *Opera*. Edited by C. Gebhardt. Heidelberg: Carl Windters Universitätsbuchhandlung.

Spinoza, B. 2002. *Complete Works*. Translated by S. Shirley, edited by M. L. Morgan. Indianapolis, IN: Hackett.

Thurschwell, A. 2005. 'Cutting the Branches for Akiba: Agamben's Critique of Derrida'. In A. Norris (ed), *Politics, Metaphysics, and Death: Essays on Giorgio Agamben's 'Homo Sacer'*. Durham, NC: Duke University Press, 173–97.

Vardoulakis, D. 2009. 'Stasis: Beyond Political Theology?'. *Cultural Critique* 73, 125–47.

Vogt, E. 2005. 'S/Citing the Camp'. In A. Norris (ed), *Politics, Metaphysics, and Death: Essays on Giorgio Agamben's 'Homo Sacer'*. Durham, NC: Duke University Press, 74–106.

Wolfson, H. A. 1969 [1934]. *The Philosophy of Spinoza*. New York: Schocken.

The Late Althusser: Materialism of the Encounter or Philosophy of Nothing?

Warren Montag

Abstract   *The 'late Althusser,' above all the posthumously published 'Underground Current of the Materialism of the Encounter,' is often regarded as a 'break' with his earlier work. The late works are read as a rejection of the 'determinism' supposedly characteristic of such texts as* For Marx *and* Reading Capital. *This essay seeks to show in contrast that a 'materialism of the encounter' is at work in the early texts, and that what is new in the late works is a return to a philosophy of origins, of an originary void as the guarantee that all that exists will pass away. There is thus a Messianism which remains the unthought residue of the late Althusser and which calls for analysis.*

And I heard, but I did not understand, and I said, 'my Lord what is the end of these?' And he said, 'go, Daniel, for the words are closed up and sealed until the time of the end'. (Daniel 12: 8–9)

The text of the 'Underground Current of the Materialism of the Encounter' poses serious challenges to anyone who seeks to read philosophical works according to the protocol initiated by Althusser himself. To read it carefully is to confront the fact that the published version consists of two sections, a short autobiographical preface and what the editor Francois Matheron describes as *'le coeur'* or core of the work (Althusser 2006: 164), some 37 pages of what appears to be an uninterrupted discourse, both excerpted by Matheron from a 142-page typed manuscript. Althusser's protocol of reading assumed that philosophical texts presented the dissimulation of coherence and consistency, not simply in order to supply to the reader what is normally expected of philosophy, but also and more importantly as a defence against the force of their own conflicts, a sort of obsessional and therefore imaginary mastery of an irreconcilable antagonism. As an 'a posteriori construction' (Althusser 2006: 163–64) to cite the words of the editor, it differs not only from texts such as 'Contradiction and Overdetermination', but even the 1970 version of 'Ideology and the Ideological State Apparatuses' which consisted, according to Althusser himself, of 'fragments of a much longer study' (Althusser 1976: 80). The latter text, although a composite, was carefully edited by Althusser and, however we may evaluate it today, exhibits a rigor and precision that is absent from 'The Underground Current' with its numerous errors of fact and attribution.

What then would justify treating this now-celebrated text written, according to Matheron, by an Althusser who was no longer Althusser, as a text at all, and to take its discrepancies as symptoms (and therefore endowed with theoretical significance) rather than mere accidents of its composition and publication? To begin to answer this unavoidable question, we might consult Althusser's own description of a work which he himself initially calls 'strange':

> As always, I have said everything in a single breath [d'un trait] trusting in some sort to the movement of a form of writing that is, as it were, 'spoken' rather than 'written'; and trusting also that readers of goodwill will meet it with something like a movement of the same kind. I have swept past [enjambant] the difficulties flagged along the way, repeated established truths when necessary, and hastened towards its end in expectation of the sequel. (Althusser 2006: 166)

The text, then, spoken in one breath, or written in one stroke, the 'condensation' as he says a few lines earlier of all he is capable of saying at that moment, hastens towards its end, but also towards an end to which there will be no sequel. As such, despite the insistence of so many readers on its novelty in relation to Althusser's earlier work, as if it marked an epistemological break internal to his own theory, 'The Underground Current' possesses the characteristics of a last testament or confession, spoken all at once, as if he were making manifest what was heretofore latent in his published oeuvre, or, perhaps more accurately, bringing what had been hidden into the open for all to see, the philosophical analogue of his autobiography.

I propose to take seriously the description of the text as a movement towards an end and to take as a starting point the problem of chronology both as it is practised and as it is theorised in the text, the sense that it is organised around an observable historical development of the idea of a 'materialism of the encounter' from its origins in Epicurus and Lucretius (with, it is true, a linking of this philosophy to that of Heidegger in order to demonstrate its contemporaneity, or rather, to demonstrate the non-contemporaneity of Heidegger whose work, as he himself insisted, marked a rejection of modernity and a return to the questions that occupied the Greeks), to Machiavelli, to the seventeenth century of Hobbes and Spinoza, to Rousseau and finally Marx. This history as presented by Althusser is all but exempt of the dramas of other such histories: it is not a time of breaks, interruptions and reversals, but a cumulative, remarkably continuous, linear time in which all that follows Epicurus and Lucretius seems little more than a progressive revelation of their doctrines as they are applied to increasingly complex historical and political problems. Of these, the most important problem is that of the origins of capitalism (and its corollary, which, as we shall see, haunts the entire narrative from start to finish, the end of capitalism).

At one point alone does the chronological organisation of the argument become itself an object of scrutiny: in the conclusion of Althusser's discussion of Spinoza, who is termed the heir to Machiavelli, he declares Hobbes to be a transitional moment between Spinoza and Rousseau. He follows this reordering of the history of philosophy with the statement that 'chronology hardly matters in the business, because each of these bodies of thought is developed for itself, despite the intermediary role played by Mersenne because what is in question is above all the resonances of a tradition buried and then revived, resonances which must be registered' (Althusser 2006: 179–80). The implication here is two-fold: (1) because each of these works is a manifestation of a buried tradition, it is not so much the development of a theory that is at issue, as the gradual excavation of what has so far remained underground; and (2) the historical or even accidental order of revelation is not therefore identical to the logical order of which the tradition is composed. In fact, Althusser's insistence that 'each of these bodies of thought developed for itself', tends to dissociate them and render relations of influence or antagonism unthinkable. But Althusser's critique of chronology remains extrinsic to the work as a whole; it is in fact, as we have noted, at odds with the organising principle of 'The Underground Current': the only exception to chronology is the inversion of Spinoza and Hobbes who were in fact contemporaries.

Why assign this lapse any importance at all? Is it not simply a lapse in rigour, a moment of confusion in an otherwise lucid text, a moment underscored by the reference to Mersenne (who died in 1648 – when Spinoza was 16) as an intermediary between Hobbes and Spinoza (which among other things suggests an association of Spinoza with Descartes for whom he is substituted in this passage)? Despite the fact that Hobbes is obviously (too obviously in fact) closer to Rousseau's doctrine than Spinoza, Althusser's chronological reversal allows him to avoid acknowledging the extent to which Spinoza's philosophy, and not just his theologico-political philosophy, represents a severe critique of Hobbes. This allows him to perform, the last thing we might have expected from Althusser, a Hobbesian reading of Spinoza, according to which, in a certain sense, Spinoza may be read as the anticipation of Hobbes, laying a metaphysical groundwork for Hobbes's political philosophy.

As if to underscore the problematisation of chronology in this text, Althusser begins his discussion of Spinoza by situating his philosophy in a period 'less than a century after Machiavelli's death' (Machiavelli died in 1527). Almost immediately, Althusser advances the thesis which he admits will appear 'paradoxical' (although, we should note, without explaining why), that 'for Spinoza, the object of philosophy is the void' (Althusser 2006: 176). Matheron inserts a note at this point in the text, informing the perhaps sceptical reader that in the very same year, 1982, Pierre Macherey 'was defending much the same paradoxical thesis' (Althusser 2006: 204) at a conference in Urbino. Before we can determine the extent to which Macherey's argument coincides with or even resembles Althusser's, we must first examine Althusser's account of the void in Spinoza.

To grasp the existence, otherwise disavowed, of the void in Spinoza's *Ethics*, we must note, Althusser contends, 'how Spinoza begins', that is, with God, although a God who is 'only nature', or 'nothing other than nature' (Althusser 2006: 176). In other words, outside of nature there is nothing, *rien*, that is, *le vide*, the void. Althusser, however, is not content merely to establish the infinity of God, but proceeds to posit the existence, outside of nature, of the void and to do so requires more than mere wordplay. To demonstrate the existence of the void as a concept in *Ethics* I, he takes up the theory of the attributes. The attributes, he tells us, can be read as a version of Epicurus' rain: they

> fall in the empty space of their determination like raindrops that can undergo encounters only in this exceptional parallelism *without encounter or union* (of body and soul ...) known as man, in this assignable but minute parallelism of thought and the body, which is still only parallelism, since here, as in all things, 'the order and connection of ideas is the same as the order and connection of things'. In sum, a parallelism without encounter, yet a parallelism that is already, in itself, encounter thanks to the very structure of the relationship between the different elements of each attribute. (Althusser 2006: 177)

Those familiar with Althusser, and more particularly with his commentary on Spinoza, will no doubt wonder at his use of *Ethics* II, Proposition 7 to support the theory of 'parallelism', a term that occurs nowhere else in Althusser's treatment of Spinoza for the very reason that it runs counter to virtually the entire of Althusser's oeuvre. In fact, it was none other than Macherey who, in his commentary on *Ethics* II, P7 reminds us that 'the parallelist reading of Proposition 7 of *de Mente* reinscribes Spinozist doctrine in a dualist perspective, explaining all of nature on the basis of the relation between extended substance and thinking substance', a position that Spinoza has 'precisely invalidated' (Macherey 1997: 73). Rather than allowing the attributes to remain extrinsic to each other even as they develop in correspondence, Spinoza explains in the scholium to the proposition that 'thinking substance and extended substance are one and the same substance' (*Ethics* II, P7, scholium). It was precisely in this spirit that Althusser himself would write in 1970 that ideas had a material existence and the consciousness was nothing other than action. Here, in 'The Underground Current', he has not only separated mind and body, but has inserted between them the infinite space of the void through which they are destined to fall in parallel for eternity.

It is possible at this point simply to dismiss Althusser's wilful distortion of Spinoza's text as a more or less clumsy attempt to cast it as a slightly disguised version of Lucretius, as if the history of 'aleatory materialism' were nothing more than a series of variations on a single theme. To do so, however, would be, in my view, a serious error; it would prevent us from understanding a concept the importance of which is not peculiar to Althusser: the concept of *le vide*, the void. This concept appears throughout the work of Althusser in diverse contexts and serves diverse and contradictory functions (Matheron 1998: 22–37; Morfino 2005: 3–6); in a sense it appears as if this entire, irreducibly complex history is staged all at once in one grand finale in 'The Underground Current'. The passage on Spinoza's theory of the attributes, described in an editorial note as nearly covered over by corrections and only barely legible, may thus be understood as a symptom, the effect of an unrecognised conflict at the heart of the text between two incompatible notions of the void.

At no point in the text is the conflictual character of the void more apparent than the following passage from the discussion of Machiavelli. Here the discussion of Machiavelli's theory of the non-accomplishment of Italy, the 'atomized country, every atom of which was descending in free fall without encountering its neighbor' (Althusser 2006: 171), moves to an exposition of the philosophy that underlies this theory. It is a philosophy which furnishes the principles that allow Althusser not so much to transform his own philosophy as to translate it into its true form, the form proper to it. Thus, 'philosophy has no object' is a 'way of saying that philosophy's "object" par excellence is nothingness, nothing or the void' [le néant, le rien ou le vide] (Althusser 2006: 174–75). When Althusser argued at an earlier point (notably in the *cours de philosophie pour scientifiques* delivered in 1967) that philosophy had no object, he was careful to specify that by this he meant that it had no object external to it. Strictly speaking, philosophy was its own object, or the element in which its own objects, philosophical objects, existed. These were the object not of a representation but of an intervention; in a striking phrase, Althusser advanced the idea that philosophy produced effects outside of itself only by intervening within itself. In its practical existence, philosophy must constantly pose to itself the question of its orientation, of the place it occupies and that which the conjuncture demands it accomplish; it must constantly ask: 'what is to be done?' Such practical questions, however, warns Althusser, can easily 're-awaken the old religious question of destiny' which is 'the mirror image of a theory of the radical "origin" of things' (Althusser 1974: 25–26). Philosophy, to be sure, must take its distance from such notions which in a sense surround and lay siege to it, but the void of a distance taken is not even a void, and the taking of a distance by drawing a line of demarcation did not even leave an empty space in its wake. In fact, Althusser concluded his course by drawing a line between himself and Rousseau and precisely warning against the theoretical effects of a certain concept of the void: 'One does not occupy a position in philosophy in the sense that Rousseau's noble savage occupies in the *Discourse on the Origin of Inequality* an *empty* corner of the forest' [un coin de forêt vide] (Althusser 1974: 116).

In 'The Underground Current', the act of demarcation, of taking a distance is substantified: the void is not practised but possessed or represented in the form of le néant, or le vide. Althusser endows philosophy, indeed, the history of philosophy with an object external to it: the nothingness that is the origin (or rather originary non-origin, a theoretical compromise which in no way escapes the implications of the concept of origins) and destiny of all things. If philosophy creates a void it does so not to occupy a space, but to unveil the heretofore concealed void that not only precedes but accompanies like a shadow all that exists as its secret and its truth. This ontological conception of the void, as we must call it, becomes for Althusser the defining characteristic, the specific difference of that 'profound tradition' (Althusser 2006: 188) that led from Epicurus to Marx. The originary void is thus at its centre, although a centre denied, repressed and forgotten by the dominant tradition which, far from neglecting these thinkers, assimilated them into itself in order better to mute their radicalism. This tradition, Althusser tells us, gave up 'thinking the origin as reason or end in order to think it as nothingness' (Althusser 2006: 188). The question for us, as we read 'The Underground

Current', is whether this now openly avowed 'theory of the radical 'origin' of things', to cite Althusser's own words, will 'reawaken the old religious question of destiny' (Althusser 1990: 82).

If Machiavelli sought to evacuate every form of providentialism and teleology from his political thought, Althusser argues, it was to reveal that the apparently teeming world of fifteenth-century Italy was in fact a void, 'every atom of which was descending in free fall without encountering its neighbor' (Althusser 2006: 171) and therefore without the possibility of the *'carambolage'*, that is, pile-up or crystallisation out of which nations, like species or worlds, could be created. In the most important sense, the sense that mattered to Machiavelli, Italy was a non-world of the non-accomplishment of the fact, the empty table awaiting the throw of the dice. If, for Machiavelli, Italy was the non-encounter among the lasting encounters of political atoms known as France and Spain, Hobbes will take the theory forward in a radical gesture that appears to abolish history, but in fact furnished its conditions of possibility. His state of nature was less the projection onto an origin of a social, historical result, that of primitive accumulation itself, the forced dissolution of rural communities and the emergence of a multitude of 'masterless men', as a figuration of the void, the originary disorder in which individuals, 'the atoms of society' sought to 'persevere in their being' like so many 'atoms descending in free fall parallel to each other' (Althusser 2006: 181). Such a condition was not simply the origin of any society no matter how lasting, it remained in abeyance but was never definitively abolished as the ever present possibility that haunted every society. It was this threat that justified and necessitated the Leviathan state.

Rousseau, in the second *Discourse*, will further refine Hobbes's theses, pointing out that Hobbes's state of nature is already a social state even if the sole social relation is one of hostility and enmity. It is therefore a pseudo-origin, not the genuine social void that must precede any society, but a counterfeit designed to justify tyranny. Rousseau, Althusser argues, returns, past the compromises that mar earlier conceptions of the state of nature associated not only with Hobbes, but even more with Locke, to 'the radical Origin of everything', that is, the state of pure nature, the 'truly radical absence of society that constitutes the essence of any possible society' (Althusser 2006: 184). What constitutes the 'radical absence of society'? Precisely the lack of any social relation, 'whether positive or negative' (Althusser 2006: 184). The 'fantastic image of the primeval forest' will serve to make palpable and conceivable the infinite void of individuals without encounters. This world without event or encounter cannot itself produce society. The conjunction of individuals can only be 'imposed' from without, by external causes that divide this infinity into contained spaces. That these atoms possess characteristics that allow them to conjoin, especially the pity that lies latent in them, awaiting only such an encounter to awaken, does not change the fact that this original condition constitutes the constant threat of the abyss into which society 'can fall back at any moment' (Althusser 2006: 186).

It is only in Althusser's discussion of Marx, to which, as he says, all his 'historical remarks are just a prelude', that the stakes of a materialism of the encounter, or more precisely, the relation of a philosophy of the void to a materialism of the encounter become apparent: 'to say that in the beginning was nothingness or disorder is to take up a position prior to any assembling and ordering' (Althusser 2006: 188). While there existed in Marx a theory of the dialectical progression of modes of production and, therefore, a theory of history as order, there coexisted with this first theory, a second, irreducibly different theory of modes of production as aleatory encounters: 'the whole that results from the taking hold of the "encounter" does not precede the "taking-hold" of its elements, but follows it; for this reason it might not have "taken hold" and a fortiori, "the encounter might not have taken place"' (Althusser 2006: 197). Capitalism might never have come into existence.

Of course, it might at this point be objected, and Althusser is well aware of this possible objection, that the fact of the possible non-accomplishment of capitalism has given way to its actual accomplishment and not simply as a brief encounter, but as one that has lasted. In fact, it has lasted longer than the time so many of its theoreticians allotted it, 'inducing stable relationships and a necessity the study of which yields "laws" – tendential laws, of course' (Althusser 2006: 197). The encounter that produces capitalism cannot be said a priori to be any less durable than that which produces nations or even biological species. It was Althusser himself who often recalled Spinoza's analysis of the durability of the Hebrew people – as aleatory a phenomenon as one could find in human history – which in certain ways was, in the typical Spinozist manner, nothing more than a metonym for the far more provocative and perhaps intolerable question of the rise to dominance and durability of Christianity itself (once the question of its truth is set aside), a question that Spinoza never directly posed, and in fact could not pose even in his correspondence (another sign of his solitude) in spite of its theologico-political urgency. In discussing this question, Althusser will have recourse to a term that would otherwise seem strangely out of place in this text: structure (Goshgarian in Althusser 2006: xli–xliii). He argues that every lasting encounter has a structure and that once the encounter takes place, there comes into being a 'primacy of the structure over its elements' (Althusser 2006: 191). Citing Lucretius and alluding less directly to Spinoza, Althusser must admit that not every atom, element or singular thing is capable not merely of 'colliding' with any other, but of becoming interlocked (he uses the verb 'accrocher') with it to form a being, a singular thing. Thus, although this order with its coherence and its laws has arisen from disorder, it is no less an order. In fact, it might well be said that this is what haunts Althusser's text: the fear of the aleatory encounter that, once established, will persist not for eternity, but, again to cite Spinoza, indefinitely, a fear of that which, in Althusser's words, *dure longtemps*, lasts a long time, that which fails to end on time, as expected and predicted. It is as a defence against even a theoretical possibility of this type that Althusser must postulate an origin, an original abyss from which all comes and to which all must return, the 'radical instability' that haunts the most interlocked structures. They too are only provisional: just as they might not have taken place they 'may no longer take place' (Althusser 2006: 174).

Interestingly, it is here, around an entire series of problems and references, that Althusser's theoretical trajectory more closely approaches Derrida's than at any other time in the history of their relationship. He reported in a letter in 1984 having recently re-read Derrida after having earlier read him 'in another context'. Derrida has led him back to Heidegger (whom he has read 'with the help of Derrida'), while Althusser has read Derrida in order to determine 'in what respect, and how he has criticized Heidegger even while basing himself on him' (Althusser 2006: 227). And although Althusser will rather quickly report having 'finished' with Heidegger ('who in the end annoyed me because of the streak of "country priest" in him' (Althusser 2006: 237)), we would be mistaken to dismiss too quickly the brief encounter between Althusser, Derrida and Heidegger. Francois Matheron has dated the first draft of 'The Underground Current' to July–September 1982; in October 1982, Derrida delivered an address at Johns Hopkins entitled 'My Chances/Mes chances: a Rendezvous with some Epicurean Stereophonies' (Derrida 1984: 1–31). The latter text, otherwise devoted to an analysis of the notion of chance in psychoanalysis, contains a brief and extremely dense reading of Heidegger (primarily section 38 of *Being and Time*) from the perspective of Epicurus and Lucretius.

It is in this context that Derrida poses a question concerning the history and function of the concept of chance that illuminates a heretofore unnoticed theme in Althusser's text, responding to it so precisely, to its words, motifs and assumptions, that Derrida might as well have been directly commenting on 'The Underground Current':

> when chance or luck are under consideration, why do the words and concepts impose the particular signification, sense, and direction of a downward movement, regardless of whether we are dealing with a throw or a fall? Why does this sense enjoy a privileged relation to the non-sense or insignificance which we find frequently associated with chance? What would such a movement of descent have to do with luck or chance? (Derrida 1984: 4–5)

Derrida's remarks call attention to Althusser's privileging of the rain as the image of atoms and of the fall [*la chute*] or falling [*tomber*] as their primary form of movement, a fact that becomes all the more noteworthy given the archival evidence that he read both Epicurus and Lucretius very closely and in the original languages. While the most frequent verb used by Epicurus to describe the motion of atoms and bodies is κινω (to move) and by Lucretius *moveo* (to move), Althusser almost exclusively describes atoms as falling. And rain has no privileged place even in Lucretius, who indeed uses the expression 'atoms raining in the void'; in *De Rerum Natura* the metaphors of rushing rivers, stormy seas, blasts of wind are far more common. At the extreme Lucretius will even, in a phrase he repeats a number of times, refer to atoms *per inane vagantur*, 'wandering through the void' (Lucretius II: ll. 83, 105, 109).

Althusser so privileges the notion of the fall as to translate the first line of Wittgenstein's *Tractatus Logico-Philosophicus, Die Welt is alles, was der Fall ist* (translated in the English edition of the work as 'The world is all that is the case') as 'the world is everything that "falls"', although modifying the translation as his sentence progresses to 'everything that comes about [*advient*], everything that is the case – by *case*, let us understand *casus*: at once occurrence and chance, that which comes about in the mode of the unforeseeable, and yet of being' (Althusser 2006: 190). The noun, *der Fall* (the case) becomes a verb '*tomber*', conjugated in the phrase '*tout ce qui "tombe"*'. It is clear Althusser regards the verb 'to fall' as the most forceful way to render the case or the event, to separate such notions from any finalism, that is, origin or end. Is Althusser correct in his assumption, or, conversely, is 'fall' linked to an entire theological and philosophical history of which Althusser takes no account and which therefore determines his text in ways that escape his knowledge and control?

The question of the fall leads Derrida from Epicurus and Lucretius to Heidegger in what he himself will call 'an admittedly violent condensation' which produces an apparently only 'fortuitous connection' (Derrida 1984: 9). He refers specifically to 'the analytic of Dasein' as discussed in Section 38 of *Being and Time*, 'Falling and Thrownness' [*Das Verfallen und die Geworfenheit*], which contains the Heideggerian motifs mobilised by Althusser: 'in Heidegger ... "things are thrown" in an inaugural "destining"''' (Althusser 2006: 191), while his philosophy '"opens up" a prospect that restores a kind of transcendental contingency of the world, into which we are "thrown"' (Althusser 2006: 170). It is here that Heidegger theorises being in the world, the '*da*' or 'there' of *Dasein* as a fallenness, and the belonging of Being to the world is conceived as '*das Verfallen des Daseins*' or the falling of *Dasein*. The 'violent condensation' of Epicurus and Heidegger proposed by Althusser and Derrida permits us to read *das Verfallen* as movement without origin, the movement by which Being becomes what it is. But, as Derrida points out in a remark that may be as relevant to Althusser as to Heidegger, Heidegger himself admits only to deny and disavow the other meaning from which the term 'fall' cannot be entirely disassociated: the 'negative evaluation' [*der negative Bewertung*], the sense of a 'fall' from a purer and higher 'primal state' [*als 'fall' einem reineren und höheren 'Urstand'*], that is, not simply or even primarily the Christian notion of the Fall, but perhaps also notions of a historically determined and therefore finite alienation (as opposed to the alienation – or inauthenticity – of Being fallen into the world), of a 'deplorable' state of which 'more advanced stages of human culture generations might be able to rid themselves' (Heidegger 1960: 220). And while Heidegger takes great pains to differentiate the Fall as he uses it from such theological and political notions, Derrida argues that 'one is all the more struck with certain analogies with such a discourse' (Derrida 1984: 9). Derrida undoubtedly refers here to the linking of *Verfallenheit* to inauthenticity; we might however apply his very brief remarks to Heidegger's (and Althusser's) discussion of Thrownness [*Geworfenheit*].

While *Geworfenheit* is a way of thinking the original dispersion of being (again for Althusser as well as for Heidegger), thrownness is not precisely synonymous with dispersion and retains a theological and anthropological cast absent from such terms as projection, propulsion, movement, etc. Similarly, for Althusser, following Heidegger's commentary in the *Letter on Humanism*, the German expression '*es gibt*' ('there is', the equivalent of '*il y a*') is no longer allowed simply to function as a postulation, but is returned to its origins in the verb '*geben*', to give: the 'there is' becomes 'it gives' and the 'it' [*es*] in the expression, Heidegger insists, is being itself. 'There is' becomes 'Being gives'. In 'The Underground Current', Althusser takes a certain distance from Heidegger's formulations, even as he deploys them: the idea that 'the world is a gift' (Althusser 2006: 170) gives way to the idea of *donner* as the dealing of cards: what is, is the *'donne primitive'*, the original deal, before which there is nothing and which thus marks the 'primacy of absence over presence' (Derrida)' (Althusser 2006: 190–91), the 'horizon which recedes endlessly before the walker' (Althusser 2006: 191). Later in the text, Althusser will return to *'es gibt'* to render it equivalent to 'there is nothing' (Althusser 2006: 190). Destiny itself (*der Geschick*, derived from the verb *'schicken'*, to send) would seem to have ceased as a concept to refer to the end and instead come to signify an inaugural or originary sending, even, as Nancy (1993) and Derrida have suggested, an originary abandonment.

The world is thus falling: it has been given (away), dealt (out), sent, abandoned, actions which the thesis of the primacy of absence over presence renders irreducible, actions before which there is nothing or no one. All of this tends to solidify and make permanent the issue and indeed the urgency of origin. 'Before the world', a phrase that is repeated throughout, the 'Underground Current', there is 'the non-world', before 'the accomplishment of the fact, its non-accomplishment'; it is precisely in the nothing that precedes what is that philosophy dwells, the eternal void in relation to which being is mere rain, fleeting condensations of matter destined quickly to dissolve. Being is not fallen, but that instantaneous falling into dissolution, into the 'nothingness and disorder' (a perfect translation of the Hebrew of the second sentence of Genesis: before creation, the world was nothingness and disorder) out of which it which it came. It is nothingness itself that declines into being, sending that which exists to its destruction. This is precisely the doctrine Hegel, in the *Phenomenology* (1970), ascribed to scepticism: everything is *'Nichtigkeit'* or nothingness. Hyppolite in his commentary suggests that this is not the epistemological scepticism of Greek and Roman antiquity, but rather that of the book accused by the Rabbinical commentators of Epicurean heresy, Ecclesiastes: all is vanity (הבל) or nothingness.[1] The sceptical consciousness 'declares the absolute vanishing' [*das Absolute Verschwinden*] and the nothingness [*Nichtigkeit*] of all things: 'Before the silver cord is snapped asunder and the golden bowl is shattered, and the pitcher is broken at the fountain, and the wheel falls shattered into the pit, and the dust returns to the earth as it was … nothingness of nothingnesses, says Koheleth, all is nothingness' (Ecclesiastes 12:6). For Althusser, however, the principle of nothingness as destiny serves not to condemn or devalue the human world in its evanescence (as is the case with Hegel's account of scepticism); it instead furnishes a principle of hope, of anticipation.

The entire principle of an originary and final nothingness is summed up in a proposition that deserves some scrutiny: 'History here is the permanent revocation of the accomplished fact by another undecipherable fact to be accomplished, without our knowing in advance whether, or when, or how the event that revokes it will come about' (Althusser 2006: 174). It is worth recalling at this point that Althusser's discussion of Spinoza ends with a reference to the prophet Daniel: here it is Althusser's own hand that inscribes the indecipherable announcement of the destruction to come, of the undoing

---

[1] In the Yiddish translation of Ecclesiastes by the great poet Yehoash, the phrase 'Vanity' is translated with the Yiddish equivalent of *'Nichtigkeit'* (נישטיקייט).

of the accomplished fact and 'the dice thrown again on the empty table' (Althusser 2006: 174). We should not be deceived by Althusser's insistence on original nothingness. The meaning of the void is here not at the moment of the encounter that 'takes hold' and produces a world, but the moment of its inevitable destruction, not the past, but the future, although a future not given to us to know, but a future to await. Is it too much to say that Althusser, writing in the 1980s, a time of defeat and despair, has thus re-written the conclusion of Benjamin's 'Theses on the Philosophy of History' (Benjamin 1968: 253–64), producing a theory of messianicity without a messiah?

But Daniel, as Althusser liked to say, following Spinoza, often did not know the meaning of his own prophecies. Is there not a meaning of the void as it is developed in this text that eludes Althusser? Indeed, if the void in 'The Underground Current' were reducible to an ontology we would be compelled to repeat to him his own words of twenty years earlier, when he could describe in a lecture to his students Foucault's *Folie et déraison* as finally unable to break with a theory of the origin as the condition of possibility of history's intelligibility. And the specific form of the origin that haunted Foucault's first great work would survive to haunt Althusser himself. That which the Althusser of 1963 could describe as a 'transcendental abyss' allowed Foucault to argue that 'the great work [*grande œuvre*] of history is indelibly accompanied by an absence of work, which renews itself at each instant, but which runs unaltered in its inevitable emptiness all throughout history: and even before history, since it is already there in the primitive decision, and after it as well since it will triumph in history's last words' (Foucault 1961: 5). 'The Underground Current' thus exhibits a strange unthought mimicry of the very 'transcendentalism' Althusser once subjected to critical scrutiny, tracking it in all its ruses through the thickets of Foucault's first major text.

To discern the existence of another notion of the void, not only irreducible to the first but actively antagonistic to it, we will return to Althusser's summary of 'the philosophy of the void': it is not only 'a philosophy which *says* that the void preexists the atoms that fall in it, but a philosophy which makes a philosophical void in order to endow itself with existence' (Althusser 2006: 174). Not only, but also: Althusser presents the two aspects of philosophy as if they were complementary, as if a philosophy that represents an ontological fact, that of the void that pre-exists all things, would serve as the foundation of the philosophy that makes a void, as if the latter's activity were to represent in discourse the former. If, however, we follow the itinerary of the statement 'philosophy makes a void', not only through this text, but through Althusser's work as a whole, we are forced to confront the fact that the work of 'evacuating all philosophical problems' cannot leave even the void itself, especially insofar as it serves as 'the radical origin of all things' (Althusser 2006: 174), untouched and unaffected.

In another symptomatic moment in the text, a moment perhaps not entirely separable from the discussion of Spinoza cited earlier, Althusser attributes the position that 'to say that in the beginning was nothingness or disorder is to take up a position prior to any assembling and ordering, and to give up thinking the origin as Reason or End in order to think it as nothingness' to a triumvirate of philosophers: Nietzsche, Deleuze and Derrida. Of the three, of course, Deleuze stands out and not only as a fellow Spinozist as Althusser once addressed him in their correspondence. For it was he, in an essay well known to Althusser, who would offer a reading of Lucretius (which could legitimately be called a Spinozist reading) which passionately contested the notion that *De rerum natura* founded its concept of nature on an originary nothingness. According to Deleuze, Lucretius, following Epicurus, rejected all previous philosophy on the grounds that it was unable to think 'nature as the production of the diverse' (Deleuze 1990: 267), seeking instead to reduce diversity to identity and to overcome difference in the name of Being or the One. It is in relation to this tendency alone that Lucretius's notion of the void may be understood: the problem with earlier philosophies is not that they lacked a conception of the void, a lack that he would attempt to fill. It was, rather, that 'because they did not want to consider the void, the void encompassed everything. Their being, their One, and their whole are artificial and unnatural, always corruptible, fleeting' (Deleuze 1990: 268). Rather than confront irreducible diversity and singularity, 'they would rather say, "being is nothing"' (Deleuze 1990: 268). At this point it is difficult not to see 'The Underground Current', at least in part, as a continuation of a philosophical tradition that, far from rejecting the void, makes of it, in however disavowed a form, the ground and truth of existence. We might even go further to see that Althusser makes explicit the all-encompassing void that earlier philosophies sought to conceal, saying out loud what they could only silently think. Is not the void for Althusser the principle which overcomes the difference between the brief and the lasting encounter, the principle in relation to which all things are resolved into the identity of pure nothingness, the origin and destiny of all things?

Indeed, Deleuze suggests that Lucretius's concept of the void functions precisely to counter the figure of an original nothingness that haunts philosophy, to empty or evacuate it, as it were, in order to allow philosophy to think the singular and the diverse. In a bold step he will declare Lucretius's *clinamen* not so much a swerve of the atom through the void as 'a kind of conatus', the persistence of a singular thing not in spite but by means of encounters and conjunctions. By thus invoking Spinoza, Deleuze points to a philosophy from which the void has already been evacuated, a philosophy whose aim is to think the infinite productivity of singularities, that is, to put it in Althusser's terms, a philosophy of the encounter without the void.

But would not the idea of a philosophy that makes a void in order to free the infinite production of the diverse and the singular from the transcendental unity imposed by the originary void mark, in its very dissociation from a reality to which it would appear to stand opposed, another form of transcendence, even a dualism of thought and extension, idea and thing, mind and body? It is at this point that Althusser's text is most in conflict with itself: the idea that philosophy does not find the void, but makes it, compels us to reverse many of the propositions Althusser advances. From this perspective, the void is not the condition of the encounter, rather, the encounter is the condition of the void, although understood as a verb, an activity rather than a substance, even if that substance is a negation of substance. In this sense, we can say of the void, as Spinoza does of God, that it does not exist prior to or outside of the encounters, conjunctions and disjunctions in which it is immanent. The void that philosophy makes would not be a constatation of the real, as if it were external to that which it represents, but rather one of its effects, a means by which it frees itself of origins and ends in order to become the infinite diversity it is, the indissociable simultaneity of thought and action that Althusser once tried to capture in the phrase 'theoretical practice' (Althusser 1969: 163–218).

Why is this other concept of the void, a concept perpetually inscribed in and on Althusser's texts, at their centre or their margins, sometimes visible, often invisible, so submerged or written over in this, Althusser's last text? Setting aside psychological explanations, we find the beginnings of a response twenty years earlier in another text whose object was the aleatory, the encounter, the singular: 'Contradiction and Overdetermination'. It was as if in that moment, a moment characterised by a balance of forces so apparently favourable to an undoing of the present, one could afford to contemplate not the dissolution to come or the void to which all would return, but, precisely, the opposite: the *'véritable blocage'*, the *'inhibition historique'* (Althusser 1969: 106) that prevented a social formation or even a mode of production from ending 'on time', that is, the time allotted to it by the theoreticians of historical evolution. How could societies that had ripened into maturity persist for so long? How could their 'decomposition' take the form of a system that could endure for decades or even centuries? Encounters of extraordinary number and variety might, it is true, bring about the destruction of a social order, but more commonly, far more commonly, such forces might serve to freeze it in place, to render it impervious to and neutralise the antagonistic forces that arise in its very effort to persist in its own being.

To situate the ontological conception of the void in the context of Althusser's corpus as a whole is then to be able to assign it its symptomatic value and force. Another text, perhaps the only other text, in which the concepts of *le vide* and *le néant* play a central role is 'The Piccolo Teatro: Bertolazzi and Brecht', published the same year as 'Contradiction and Overdetermination' and which shares many of the concerns mentioned a moment ago. What is striking about these terms in this early text is that they are the concepts that allow Althusser to think another time than that of the encounter that strikes like lightening in the void. They are the concepts of an 'empty time' [*d'un temps vide*], 'a time empty of events and collisions', a time 'long and slow to live', a time in which a structure formed by an encounter long since forgotten remains silent and immobile (Althusser 1969: 134; translation modified). It is 'a time in which nothing happens', nothing that is, that can be called an event, 'a time without hope or future, a time in which the past itself is frozen in repetition' (Althusser 1969: 135–36; translation modified). It is a 'time in which gestures have neither result nor effect', not because the effects are doomed immediately to pass away, but because there are no effects. It is a time of 'unbearable vacuity' [*d'une vacuité insoutenable*]. When will the event that in an instant shatters this world of empty repetition occur? Only 'when everyone has departed', for its time is irreducibly foreign to the time of nothingness. This play, like those of Brecht, subjects the 'illusions of consciousness' to the experience of an intolerable temporality: 'thus, in Galileo the history that is slower than the consciousness impatient for truth, the history which is also disconcerting for a consciousness never able to "grasp" it durably in the time of its short life' (Althusser 1969: 143). 'The Underground Current', then, is the chronicle of 'a waiting that knows itself in vain' (Beckett 1991: 241), for a future that does not arrive late or on time, of a consciousness that confuses its time with the time of history, and its end with the end of a mode of production, unwilling and perhaps unable to grasp the fact that from the perspective of a genuine materialism of the encounter, just as nothing guarantees the arrival of the best, so nothing absolutely prohibits the endurance of the worst.

References

Althusser, L. 1969. *For Marx.* Translated by B. Brewster. London: Verso.

Althusser, L. 1974. *Philosophie et la philosophie spontanée des savants.* Paris: Maspero.

Althusser, L. 1976. *Positions.* Paris: Editions Sociales.

Althusser, L. 1990. *Philosophy and the Spontaneous Philosophy of the Scientists.* Translated by W. Montag. London: Verso.

Althusser, L. 2006. *Philosophy of the Encounter: Later Writings, 1978–1987.* Translated by G. M. Goshgarian. London: Verso.

Beckett, S. 1991. *Three Novels.* New York: Grove Press.

Benjamin, W. 1968. *Illuminations.* New York: Schocken.

Deleuze, G. 1990. 'Lucretius and the Simulacrum'. In *The Logic of Sense.* New York: Columbia, 266–79.

Derrida, J. 1984. 'My Chances/Mes chances: a Rendezvous with some Epicurean Stereophonies'. In J. H. Smith and W. Kerrigan (eds), *Taking Chances: Derrida, Psychoanalysis and Literature.* Baltimore: Johns Hopkins University Press, 1–32.

Foucault, M. 1961. *Folie et déraison: l'histoire de le folie à l'âge classique.* Paris: Gallimard.

Hegel, G. W. F. 1970. *Phänomenology des Geistes.* Frankfurt: Suhrkamp.

Heidegger, M. 1960. *Sein und Zeit.* Tübingen: Max Niemeyer Verlag.

Macherey, P. 1997. *Introduction à l'Éthique de Spinoza. La seconde partie: la réalité mentale.* Paris: Presses Universitaires de France.

Matheron, F. 1998. 'The Recurrence of the Void in Louis Althusser'. *Rethinking Marxism* 10:3, 22–37.

Morfino, V. 2005. 'An Althusserian Lexicon', *Borderlands* 4:2. Available online: http://www.borderlands.net.au/vol4no2_2005/morfino_lexicon.htm (accessed 12 January 2010).

Nancy, J.-L. 1993. 'Abandoned Being'. In *The Birth to Presence.* Translated by B. Holmes et al. Stanford, CA: Stanford University Press, 36–47.

Naming the Nothing: Nancy and Blanchot on Community

Ian James

Abstract   *This article examines the exchange between Jean-Luc Nancy and Maurice Blanchot around the question of community. It argues that Nancy from the early 1980s onwards offers an understanding of community as an exposure to, or of, a nothing or empty space. This nothing or empty space can be understood as the space left vacant by the withdrawal of any transcendent principle which would underpin or guarantee various forms of political organization or historical becoming. Whether it be the absence of any divine principle which would legitimate monarchical or imperial authority, or the absence of any essence or goal for the human in history (e.g. the bonds of national community or communism), the 'nothing' of community is exposed in the wake of the withdrawal or retreat of political transcendence.*

Blanchot's response to Nancy's essay 'La Communauté désœuvrée', entitled La Communauté inavouable *is critical of Nancy's thinking on this subject but, this article argues, he is critical only insofar as he shares with Nancy the problem of thinking, naming, or exposing the 'nothing' of community. The difference of these two key French thinkers about this question reminds us that ethical and political stakes of thinking community in the absence of metaphysical ground are always a matter of thinking community as absence. It also remind us that this thinking of community occurs in the experience of the 'community of writing.'*

The current state of the world is not a war of civilizations. It is a civil war. (Jean-Luc Nancy, *La Communauté affrontée*)

Nearly twenty years after the publication of his essay 'La Communauté désœuvrée' (Nancy 1983; translated as *The Inoperative Community* 1991a), Jean-Luc Nancy returned to the question of community in a short work entitled *La Communauté affrontée* (Nancy 2001; translated as 'The Confronted Community' 2003a). In French the verb 'affronter' means to face, confront, or to clash with an enemy or adversary. At the beginning of the twenty-first century, Nancy suggests in this short work, our world is one which is 'tearing itself apart' [*qui se déchire*]. It is a global community which 'is separated from and in confrontation with itself' [*qui est séparée et affrontée à elle-même*] (Nancy

2001: 17).[1] The opening sentence of *La Communauté affrontée*, however, firmly distances itself from Samuel Huntington's widely known argument relating to the 'clash' of civilisations (Huntingdon 1996): 'The current state of the world is not a war of civilizations. It is a civil war' (Nancy 2001: 11). The contemporary global community may be divided from itself in the mode of clash or confrontation, Nancy contends, but this is more an internecine war than it is one of separate civilisations confronting each other across discrete cultural boundaries. Yet this is a civil war of a rather singular and perhaps unprecedented kind. The community of 'globalisation' is not one in dispute over the identity of values or over a possible shared destiny which would be common to all. Rather, Nancy contends, it is a community divided, separated and confronting itself over a gaping abyss. Or, more precisely, it is a community which *is* an abyss, a community which 'is gaping – gaping open over its own unity and over its absent essence – and which confronts this rupture within itself' (Nancy 2001: 17).

In this singular invocation of a civil war dividing global community from itself, Nancy is offering a philosophical account of a specific historical trajectory and a specific historical outcome which, he contends, characterises the beginning of the twenty-first century. 'What is happening to us is an exhaustion of the thinking of the One and of a unique destination of the world: the world is exhausting itself in a unique absence of destination' (Nancy 2001: 12). Where once national, cultural or religious communities might have thought of themselves as distinct and fought or clashed over the future preeminence of their respective value systems and world views, what now characterises a community become global, or a community of globalisation defined only by its extension across the finite space of the globe itself, is an absence of value, of destiny or destination. For Nancy: 'The gaping abyss [*béance*] which is formed is that of sense, of truth or of value' (Nancy 2001: 13). What is at stake here is the impossibility of global community being able to affirm a shared essence or goal by which it might define itself in terms of identity or self-presence.[2]

Writing nearly twenty years after the publication of 'La communauté désœuvrée' and fifteen years after the publication of the full-length volume bearing the same title, Nancy appears, in 2001, to be re-inscribing the 'unworked' community of the earlier text into the contemporary historical context of post-cold war globalisation and conflict.[3] As in the earlier text,

---

[1] All translations of Nancy's works cited herein are mine.

[2] One might immediately object to Nancy here that the years following the end of the Cold War have not lacked an affirmation of a shared global destiny, which is to say, that of capitalism, free trade, and liberal democracy. It might be noted, however, that such an affirmation has been the preserve of elites and governments of specific countries, albeit countries with a certain global dominance. The gap that exists between such affirmations of a shared, liberal, capitalist destiny and the reality of the global community (its contemporary existence and unverifiable future) may, quite precisely, be the site of the empty space or '*béance*' about which Nancy writes.

[3] Clearly *La Communauté affrontée* is written very much with its contemporary resonance in mind. An full exploration of this is beyond the scope of this discussion insofar as the relation between Nancy and Blanchot is the central point of focus here.

community is recast not as the intimate sharing of an essence or identity but rather as the opening of an absence of identity in the spacing of a shared finitude. In both cases, community is an exposure to, or of, a nothing or empty space. This nothing or empty space can be understood as the space left vacant by the withdrawal of any transcendent principle which would underpin or guarantee various forms of political organisation or historical becoming. Whether it be the absence of any divine principle which would legitimate monarchical or imperial authority, or the absence of any essence or goal for the human in history (e.g. the bonds of national community or communism), the 'nothing' of community is exposed in the wake of the withdrawal or retreat of political transcendence.[4] This nothing or empty space cannot be recuperated into the 'work' of any communal identity or shared destiny. At the same time 'absence' here (of essence, of theological principle etc.) cannot, as will become clear, be opposed to 'presence' insofar as it is affirmed by Nancy as an originary absence which functions as a condition of possibility (and impossibility) of any experience of community at all. The key issue here will be the manner in which Nancy (and also Blanchot) seeks to affirm or think the absence of community as that which is always already anterior to community itself, experienced either as presence or plenitude (of shared essence/divine principle) *or* as the loss of presence or plenitude and a nostalgic attempt to recuperate that loss.

In *La Communauté affrontée*, then, the ontology of unworked community developed in the early 1980s in response to the question of the 'end of communism' has become the contemporary being of a global community riven from itself. What marks a clear difference in these two moments of Nancy's thinking about community is the emphasis on war or conflict. In the earlier texts the 'unworking' of community as identity or as an intimate sharing of essence was clearly set against a broader thinking of totalitarianism thought by Nancy according to a logic of 'immanence'.[5] In the later text, the absence at the heart of community is the condition for its division from itself, or rather it is its very existence *as* division, separation, clash or self-confrontation. The exhaustion of value, of a unitary historical destiny for the global community, leaves only the abyssal opening of an empty space.

The question of the nothing is posed in Nancy's philosophical thinking about community in works separated by an interval of nearly twenty years. In fact, it is arguable that the different ways of thinking, naming or responding to the nothing of community strongly inflects the development and trajectory of Nancy's thinking over this period. This problem of thinking the nothing is posed very explicitly by Nancy himself at the beginning of *La Communauté affrontée*: 'How can the nihil be thought without being returned to an all-powerful and all-present monstrosity?' (Nancy 2001: 13). The reference here to all-powerful and all-present monstrosity recalls, albeit obliquely, Nancy's

---

[4] Of crucial importance here are the analyses given of political transcendence and of the 'retreat of the political' by Lacoue-Labarthe and Nancy in the Centre for Philosophical Research on the Political. See *Le Retrait du Politique* (Nancy & Lacoue-Labarthe 1983: 192–93), *Retreating the Political* (Nancy & Lacoue-Labarthe 1997: 129).

[5] For an extended discussion of this see James, *The Fragmentary Demand: An Introduction to the Philosophy of Jean-Luc Nancy* (2006: 173–93).

earlier philosophical account of totalitarianism in *La Communauté désœuvree*, that is, totalitarianism as a project of immanence in which a figure of shared identity would be 'put to work' in order to define the collective 'being-together' and future destiny of a political community. Nancy recalls the terms of this account of immanence more explicitly slightly later in his discussion: 'All powerfulness and omnipresence, is always what is required of community or what is sought in it: sovereignty and intimacy, self-presence without flaws and without exteriority' (Nancy 2001: 15). What is at stake in the question of the nothing, or the thinking of the 'nihil,' is the very meaning and essence of community itself: how can community be thought at all without being recuperated into totalising figures of identity, without returning to the violence and potential monstrosity of a totalising project? How can absence be thought prior to the opposition of presence-absence and therefore outside of any dialectical logic which would recuperate absence into a totalising figure of overarching presence?

It might be worth noting at this point that the main section of *La Communauté affrontée* was, in fact, first published as a preface to a new Italian edition of Maurice Blanchot's *La Communauté inavouable* (Blanchot 1983; 1988). *La Communauté affrontée* as a whole is dedicated to Blanchot and offers a contextualisation of, and a further response to, Blanchot's short 1983 work, itself a response to Nancy's original essay, 'La Communauté désœuvrée.' This is worth noting because it is perhaps precisely around the problem of thinking, naming, or exposing the 'nothing' that the exchange between Nancy and Blanchot on the question of community takes place. In the original essay, Nancy unfolds his critique of traditional identitarian models of community in the light of the historical experience of Germany under National Socialism and in the context of George Bataille's affirmation of a 'sacrificial community' in the 1930s. As has already been indicated, totalitarianism is thought in this context as 'immanence' and describes an experience of 'communal fusion,' that is to say, of organic communion of community with itself in which an intimate communication of an identity and future destiny would occur (Nancy 1985: 30–33; 1991a: 9–11). In order to think community outside its traditional model and outside figures of fusion, totality and immanence, Nancy draws on Heidegger's thinking of 'being-with' as developed in *Sein und Zeit* and on Bataille's thinking of sacrifice, communication, sovereignty, and excess as developed in the 1930s and after.[6] In particular, Nancy takes up Bataille's affirmation that 'Sovereignty is NOTHING' in order to articulate an understanding of community as a fundamental 'being-with' of finite beings in excess of any project or work of identity. It is in this crossing of the language of Heideggarian finitude with that of Bataillian sovereignty that Nancy's initial thinking of the nothing of community unfolds. It is precisely this crossing of Heidegger with Bataille, however, which sets the terms for the subsequent exchange which occurs between Nancy and Blanchot around the avowability or unavowability of the 'nothing.'

---

[6] Nancy's work on the question of community has perhaps received more commentary than any other aspect of his work. Amongst the most important of these responses are: Simon Critchley (1993), Fraser (1984), Ingram (1988), Norris (2000), Readings (1989). See also Ian James, 'On Interrupted Myth' (James 2005).

In *La Communauté affrontée* Nancy describes the context surrounding the original publication of 'La Communauté désœuvrée' and comments also on Blanchot's subsequent response. That response, he suggests:

> was at once an echo, a resonance, a reply, a reservation, and even, in a certain way, a reproach.

> I have never completely clarified this reservation or reproach, neither in a text, nor for myself, nor in correspondence with Blanchot. (Nancy 2001: 38)

It may well be that the exact or full nature of this reproach will remain rather obscure or impossible to clarify in its entirety. The opening of *La Communauté inavouable* suggests that Blanchot's own engagement with the question of community has, for him, been a matter of 'uninterrupted questioning' (Blanchot 1988: 2). If a reproach is made in this work, it relates, in a rather private way perhaps, to Blanchot's own thought and itinerary, and perhaps also to his shared experience and friendship with Bataille. Certainly the reading of Bataille that Blanchot offers in *La Communauté inavouable* diverges in key respects from the reading offered by Nancy in 'La Communauté désœuvrée'. In his original essay, Nancy draws on Bataille in a number of ways in order to think a fundamental being-with outside of any figure or project of identity or communal belonging (see James 2006: 179–86). Yet he is critical of Bataille in a number of ways also. On the one hand Nancy suggests that Bataille's commitment to the notion of a sacrificial community, embodied most clearly in his activity around the secret society of *Acéphale*, resulted in failure and, by implication, brought him also into a dangerous proximity with the project of National Socialism (Nancy 1985: 46–47; 1991a: 17). At the same time, Nancy criticises Bataille for retaining a Hegelian language of subject and object in his account of 'communication' and of sacrificial community as a shared exposure to death (Nancy 1991a: 23–24). The language of ecstatic self-dispossession and of fusion which characterises Bataille's singular understanding of 'communication' again runs the risk, Nancy implies, of repeating a logic of identity and therefore of repeating a fusional, immanentist model of community at the very moment it aims to think beyond such a model (Nancy 1991a: 17).

For his part, Blanchot contests the terms and substance of Nancy's reading of Bataille and in so doing he also contests the terms in which Nancy comes to think community in general. For Blanchot, Bataille's affirmation of sacrificial community, and in particular, his activity around the 'secret society' of *Acéphale*, cannot be seen as a *project*, that is, as an attempt to inaugurate or embody a sacrificial community. Not being a project of 'embodying' community, the secret society of *Acéphale* cannot be judged by the criteria of success or failure or be compared (even obliquely) to other attempts to embody community (for example, that of National Socialism). For Blanchot, Bataille's affirmation of the secret society of *Acéphale* was not an attempt to re-embody a sacrificial community but, rather, an attempt to affirm an absent community, or rather to affirm community *as* absence:

> The absence of community is not the failure of community: it belongs to community in its extreme moment or as the test which exposes its necessary disappearance. *Acéphale* was the common experience of that which cannot be placed in common, not properly maintained, nor reserved for an ulterior abandon ... The community of *Acéphale* could not exist as such, but only as imminence and as withdrawal. (Blanchot 1988: 15)

It is in this context that the meaning of Blanchot's use of the term 'unavowable', as opposed to 'unworked', becomes clearer. For Blanchot, the experience of 'absent' community is not something which can be either worked or unworked or thought dialectically or oppositionally in relation to any possible instance of presence. Since its existence is only ever, and always already, one of absence and withdrawal, it exists prior to any possibility of dialectical working and unworking, and, indeed, prior to any logic of existence or being at all. It exists, as it were, only in and *as* nothing.

The reservation or reproach that Blanchot expresses in relation to Nancy's reading of Bataille and to his thinking of community as 'unworked' appears, in part at least, to relate to the language of being-with or existence (that is to say, to the language of ontology) which Nancy uses to 'avow' the nothing of community. As has been pointed out by a number of commentators, Blanchot, in *La Communauté inavouable*, explicitly rejects ontology in favour of an account of the ethical relation which appears heavily indebted to Levinas:

> Ethics is only possible if ontology – which always reduces the Other to the Same – gives way, and can affirm an anterior relation in which the self is not content simply to recognize the Other, to recognize itself in the Other, but is placed in question by it to the point where the self can only respond through a responsibility which cannot be limited and which exceeds it without being exhausted. (Blanchot 1988: 43)[7]

For Blanchot, it appears crucial to mark the 'absence of community' as a withdrawal and as anterior to being and any logic of presence. That 'extreme moment' of community where the fusion, identity or substance of community itself disappears must be marked as a withdrawal from being or more precisely as an alterity which would be prior to any horizon or logic of 'being-with'. The relation to the 'nothing' of community is one which precedes ontology and so must be affirmed, not as the 'unworking' of community but, rather, as its unavowability.

Blanchot, then, is not only offering a different account of Bataille, of his affirmation of sacrificial community, and of his activity around the secret

---

[7] This question has been dealt with excellently by Leslie Hill who gives a brief account of the exchange between Nancy and Blanchot in *Maurice Blanchot: Extreme Contemporary* (1996: 200–4). See also Stella Gaon's excellent account of the question of ontology versus ethics in Blanchot and Nancy: 'Communities in Question: Sociality and Solidarity in Nancy and Blanchot' (2005).

society of *Acéphale*. He is also refusing the crossing of Heideggerian and Bataillian language and terminology which Nancy uses to articulate the unworking of community. The reproach of *La Communauté inavouable* may well relate not just to the way in which Nancy criticises Bataille, but also to the way in which he persists with Heidegger and with the Heideggarian language of being. If Nancy reads an unthought proximity of the Bataillian fusional language of 'communication' to that other fusional language, that is, the immanentist language of the National Socialist community, one might suggest that Blanchot returns the compliment by implying that the violence implicit in the language of ontology is also historically and philosophically compromised (Blanchot 1983: 27; 1988: 13).

The exchange between Blanchot and Nancy appears to resolve itself into a question of naming or avowal. For Blanchot, the 'nothing' of community, its absence or withdrawal, is not nameable, avowable or presentable as such. He puts this problem in the following terms:

> Does that mean that community does not avow itself or that there is no avowal which will reveal [community] since, in each moment that its manner of being has been talked about, one feels that one has seized that manner of being in the absence of that which makes it exist? Would it have been better then to remain silent? ... in the final analysis, in order to remain silent it is necessary to speak. But with what kind of words? (Blanchot 1988: 56)

Perhaps the distance which separates Nancy and Blanchot on the question of community is, in fact, a matter of words, a matter of choosing the right words in order to mark an absence, empty space, or opening onto nothing. This distance, then, amounts to very little. It is a difference in philosophical or rhetorical strategy, a difference in gesture. If the distance that separates Blanchot and Nancy here is simply a matter of words, if the unworked and the unavowable affirm differently an opening of community onto and as nothing, then Nancy's frustration, his lack of clarity in relation to Blanchot's reproach, might seem quite understandable. They are, after all, trying to say the same thing in different terms. Or rather, they are both trying to think an instance, that is, an originary absence or withdrawal of essence which escapes any logic of the same. If one were to remark, for instance, that Nancy's absence or nothing is not at all the same kind of absence or nothing that is affirmed by Blanchot, this would make little sense, since such an absence cannot possibly be designated by a concept. No concept would be equal or equivalent to the instance, anterior to all conceptuality, which is being impossibly designated. What is important is the gesture or terms by which such an impossible affirmation is made. The key point to underline here is that both Blanchot and Nancy seek to affirm the difference of community from itself, its withdrawal from substance, identity and presence, through different gestures. It is the specificity of these gestures which needs to be explored since, as Nancy himself concedes, the stakes are in fact very high where it is a question of: 'How ... the nihil [can] be thought without being returned to an all-powerful and all-present monstrosity?' (Nancy 2001: 13). He outlines these stakes further towards the very end of *La Communauté affrontée*:

there is a task, the task of daring to think the unthinkable, to think that which cannot be assigned, the untreatable of being-with, to think it without submitting it to any hypostasis. It is not a political task nor an economic task, it is altogether more serious and it governs the full extent of both the political and the economic. (Nancy 2001: 50)

The task of thought then again asserts itself in the most serious terms. Thinking the nothing of community carries with it the task of thinking the political beyond or in excess of its traditional metaphysical foundations and beyond those traditional grounding figures or myths by which community has traditionally sought to embody or instantiate itself as substance, as intimacy, and as the communication or sharing of an essence.

This much, then, is clear. Blanchot and Nancy disagree about the mode or gesture by which the nothing of community might be named, about the mode or gesture by which its unavowability might be affirmed. What is perhaps less clear, and remains to be clarified yet further, is the exact nature of Nancy's gesture, the exact manner in which he deploys the language of ontology, and whether this can be reduced in any straightforward manner to any kind of (albeit reformed) Heideggerianism. Nancy's initial response to Blanchot is illuminating in this regard. When *La Communauté désœuvrée* was published as a full-length work in 1986, the original essay that appeared in *Aléa* was supplemented with four further essays: on myth, on 'literary communism', on being-in-common, and on finite history. The original essay was also supplemented with a note which refers to Blanchot's book and indicates quite explicitly that the essay on myth in the full-length version represents 'another way' of 'prolonging further the 'uninterrupted reflection' of Blanchot' on the question of community (Nancy 1991a: 42). Nancy also affirms that this is a reflection which itself cannot be interrupted, a reflection which has been prolonged by many names other than Blanchot and Bataille in many different texts too numerous to name or avow:

> … interwoven, alternating, shared texts, offering, like all texts, that which belongs to no one and which returns to every one: the community of writing, the writing of community. (Nancy 1991a: 42)

Nancy's invocation of writing and the anonymity of 'no one' here is perhaps significant. His alignment of community with writing and anonymity might suggest that his initial response to Blanchot's text is to stress the *proximity* of his own thinking and writing with that of Blanchot. Certainly this would be born out in the emphasis on interruption and literary communism in the essays which follow, both of which could arguably be said to prolong or reinscribe key Blanchottian concerns relating to community and the question of the political.

Nancy's emphasis on the proximity of his thinking to that of Blanchot is perhaps not misplaced. Despite Blanchot's reproach, and despite the apparent distance between the two writers on the question of ontology, it is worth highlighting the extent to which Nancy's formulations in the original essay of 'La Communauté désœuvrée' deploy the language of ontology in a very specific manner. In this context, Blanchot's comment in *La Communauté inavouable*, that ontology 'always reduces the Other to the Same' (1988: 60) is, at the very least, open to question. Community, Nancy writes in the original essay: 'Is the presentation of finitude and the excess without return which makes [*qui font*] finite being' (Nancy 1991a: 15). The emphasis placed here on finitude and on finite being clearly repeats the terms of the Heideggerian thinking of being. The reference to the 'excess without return' of finite being could easily be interpreted also as a repetition of the earlier Heidegger's thinking of ontological difference (the thought that being cannot be reduced to, and is always in excess of, beings). Yet the reference to excess also, of course, recalls Bataille's thinking. It is here that closer attention needs to be paid to the 'crossing' of a Heideggerian and Bataillian language alluded to earlier in this discussion.

It is precisely around the 'nothing' of Bataillian sovereignty that this crossing of terms or idiom is most insistent in Nancy's text:

> 'Sovereignty is NOTHING.' That is to say that sovereignty is the sovereign exposure to an excess (to a transcendence) which does not present itself, does not let itself be appropriated (nor simulated), which does not even *give* itself – an excess to which being is abandoned rather. The excess to which sovereignty is exposed and exposes us *is* not, in a sense perhaps close to that in which Heideggerian Being 'is not'. (Nancy 1991a: 18)

The terms Nancy uses here are slightly different from those used by Blanchot to characterise the 'absent community' of *Acéphale*, and yet the proximity between the two is striking. The 'absence of community', it might be recalled, was, for Blanchot, 'the common experience of that which cannot be placed in common, not properly maintained, nor reserved for an ulterior abandon … The community of *Acéphale* could not exist as such, but only as imminence and as withdrawal' (Blanchot 1988: 15). Nancy's excess, which cannot be appropriated or simulated and to which being is abandoned, is surely also nothing which can be: 'maintained, nor reserved for an ulterior abandon'. It is not an excess reserved and then abandoned *by* being, but one to which being is, as it were, always already abandoned. Likewise, one might wonder whether Blanchot's invocation of absence as 'imminence and withdrawal' is really so different from Nancy's invocation of an excess which 'is not'. In both cases the nothing of community is withdrawn from existence as an irreducible alterity or excess. The proximity of Nancy's formulations to those of Blanchot is affirmed even further elsewhere in 'La Communauté désœuvrée' when, for instance, he weaves the language of excess and of the nothing in with the distinctly Blanchottian motif of the 'outside' [*le dehors*]. He does this when speaking of the 'rending apart' [*déchirure*] of singular being in 'unworked community':

> The rending apart consists only in an exposure to the outside: all the 'outside' of singular being is exposed to the 'outside' … There is not a rending apart of nothing, with nothing; rather there is a compearance to NOTHING. (Nancy 1991a: 30)

It might be clear from this that Nancy does not restrict himself exclusively to a crossing of Bataille with Heidegger in his attempt to think the nothing, absence, or unworking of community in 'La Communauté désœuvrée'. This nothing is named in a number of ways: as 'sovereign excess' (Bataille), as finite transcendence (Lacoue-Labarthe), as an excess that 'is not' (Heidegger and ontological difference), as the outside (Blanchot), as 'déchirure', but also, elsewhere, as clinamen and as the unidentifiable (Nancy 1991a: 6).[8]

One might conclude from this that Nancy's gesture in 'La Communauté désœuvrée' is not simply to repeat in a slightly reformed manner the Heideggerian thinking of 'being-with' by re-inscribing *Mitsein* as more funda-mental than *Dasein* on the one hand, and by bringing it into contact with Bataille's thinking about communication on the other. Rather, he is engaging in a writerly strategy in which a range of different terms are deployed and woven together in order to expose his thinking of community to the nothing. If, in his note responding to Blanchot in the full-length edition of *La Commu-nauté désœuvrée*, Nancy invokes 'the community of writing, the writing of community' as a series of 'interwoven, alternating, shared texts' (Nancy 1991a: 42), it is arguable that his original essay was already an affirmation of that community of writing. The nothing of community is named in Nancy's original essay only in just such an interweaving, alternating and sharing of diverse terms. But the nothing, in a sense, is named only in the space or the distance between these terms rather than in a logic of continuity or sameness that would bind them together. In this multiple naming, the nothing of community is at the same time placed in excess of any name, it is avowed, as it were, only in the affirmation of its 'umasterable excess', only in its very unavowability.[9]

This is worth noting for a number of reasons. Firstly, it suggests that although Blanchot may or may not be right to correct Nancy's reading of Bataille, his implicit reproach in relation to Nancy's persistence with ontology and with a Heideggerian thinking of being misconstrues the nature of the rhetorical and writerly strategy adopted in 'La Communauté désœuvrée'. Nancy is not simply repeating and 'reforming' Heidegger's thinking of being as a more fundamental being-with, and, crucially, he is not seeking to retrieve or enclose absence or nothing within the logos of an ontological discourse. The Heideggerian idiom enters into a resonance with a range of other non-Heideggerian terms and can only be read in relation to its resonance with those terms. This, then, is a community of writing which turns around the very nothing of community itself, and in that play something else emerges: a thinking of the 'exposure' or sharing of singular being which *is* otherwise than Heideggerian being. This is a thinking which emerges from a sharing of

---

[8] 'Clinamen' is a term in used in the atomistic philosophy of Lucretius to describe the manner in which atoms 'swerve' towards each other when falling: it therefore both suggests separation or spacing and the possibility of relation or contact. Inevitably, then, the clinamen offers a useful figure for a void or nothing which nevertheless creates the possibility of relationality between singular instances.

[9] This looks forward to Nancy's later thinking of 'exscription', the motif he uses to describe an excess over what is written or, as Nancy himself puts it: 'writing is *exscribed*, places itself outside of the sense that it inscribes, in the things of which writing is supposed to form the inscription. And this exscription is the final truth of inscription' (Nancy 1997a: 79).

thought within a community of writing in which, precisely, nothing is shared, or in which there is a shared exposure to the nothing (Bataille, Blanchot, Lacoue-Labarthe and, amongst others, Antelme and Derrida). Secondly, Nancy's strategy of repeating terms by interweaving, alternating and sharing them with other terms from other texts is worthy of note because it inflects the nature of his philosophical idiom as it develops in the period of the 1980s, 1990s and after. If Blanchot's reproach relates to the persistence of ontology in the thinking of unworked community, then he may be aligned with those, often highly influential, commentators who have judged Nancy to be too Heideggerian, too wedded to the language of finite being, or, in other ways, far too willing to retain specific traditional and highly value-laden philosophical terms.[10]

It is arguably always rather reductive to characterise Nancy as 'Heideggerian' in any orthodox sense, and certainly his use of the language of finite being and finitude needs to be set in the context of the strategy of interweaving, alternating and sharing terms described above. Certainly he does persist with the language of ontology and finitude in his major works of the 1980s and 1990s (*L'Expérience de la liberté* (1988; translated as *The Experience of Freedom* 1993b), *Une pensée finie* (1990; translated as *A Finite Thinking* 2003b), *La Comparution* (1991b), *Le Sens du monde* (1993a; translated as *The Sense of the World* 1997c) and *Être singulier pluriel* (1997b; translated as *Being Singular Plural* 2000) to name the most obvious examples). Yet he does so within the demand that ontology be fundamentally refigured, as he puts it in *Être singulier pluriel*: 'with a thorough resolve that starts *from the singular-plural of origins*, from being-with' (Nancy 2000: 26). This is a task which, as has been suggested, begins at least as early as 1983 with the publication of 'La Communauté désœuvrée', where being-with is thought only in terms of a rending of singular being, its exposure to the nothing or to the excess of an 'outside'.

As Nancy's refiguring of ontology develops from the early through to the late 1990s, the crossing of the language of finite being with other idioms becomes more and more pronounced. In *La Comparution* (1991b) the commitment to an ontology of being-with is repeated and developed further in the term 'compearance' and in terms which both repeat but also move beyond Heidegger (Nancy 1991b: 57, 65). At this stage, Nancy still retains the language of the excess of finite existence but comes also to stress very heavily the notion of 'common space'. It is the 'emptiness the opening of this space, its very spacing or numerous spacings, which form the place of our compearance' (Nancy 1991b: 53). Once again, community is figured as an opening onto, or spacing of, an absence of essence or identity, the nothing of community is named as emptiness [*le vide*]. The term 'compearance' is mentioned only briefly in 'La Communauté désœuvrée', but by 1991 it has come to supplant the terminology of working and unworking as the dominant figure in Nancy's thinking of being-with. It is clear that the language Nancy uses to

---

[10] This criticism has been made explicitly, for instance, by Simon Critchley (1993). Many of Derrida's critical remarks on Nancy, like those of Blanchot, also question the philosophical terms or language which Nancy chooses to retain; see Derrida *Le Toucher, Jean-Luc Nancy* (Derrida 2000; translated as *On Touching – Jean-Luc Nancy* 2005a), and *Voyous* (Derrida 2003; translated as *Rogues* 2005b).

name the nothing of community never remains static, it is always shifting, mobile and plural. This can been seen quite clearly in the second half of the 1990s when Nancy's philosophical language changes once again and undergoes a potentially decisive shift.

1997 sees the publication of two major works by Nancy: *Être singulier pluriel* (Nancy 1997b) and *Hegel: L'Inquiétude du négatif* (Nancy 1997d; translated as *Hegel: The Restlessness of the Negative* 2002). The former is clearly a very significant work insofar as it marks a major step in the development of Nancy's 'refigured' ontology and represents a major contribution to recent European philosophy more generally. The latter text might appear, at first glance, to be of rather less importance, published as it is by Hachette in a series of short monographs on diverse figures ranging from philosophers and writers to artists and figures from popular culture (Deleuze, Mallarmé, Flaubert and Melville appear on the series list, along with Klee and Picasso, but also with Hergé and Buster Keaton). Yet, despite the scope of the series in which the Hegel text appears, it arguably marks a decisive moment in Nancy's thinking, a certain shift or turn which resonates into his works of the late 1990s and into his more recent work at the beginning of the twenty-first century.

Nancy stresses in the cover notes to *L'Inquiétude du négatif* that his short work is not intended to be, nor can it succeed in being, a simple gloss on 'Hegelianism', nor a restitution of Hegel's thinking. Rather, he insists, its aim is to read Hegel, to 'think' Hegel 'such as he has been reread or rethought by us up until now, such as he has already been played out in thinking' (Nancy 2002: 7). This is not a simple exegesis of the Hegelian text, therefore, but, rather, a rereading of Hegel which occurs in the wake of, and can only be understood in the light of, a prior (largely French) tradition of interpretation.[11] What emerges from Nancy's reading is not a Hegel for whom the operations of dialectical thought and the thinking of 'absolute knowledge' constitute a desire for totalisation. This is not Hegelianism viewed as a totalising gesture by which difference and alterity would be appropriated by the logic of the Same.[12] This is a Hegel for whom the negative, or the 'work' of negativity, represents a ceaseless restlessness which ruptures temporality and the presencing or presentation of the present. Negativity, here, does not determine the finite present through the work of concrete negation, rather, it traverses existence in a manner which exposes it to the instability of any and all finite determination. Once again, Nancy engages in a rather complex crossing of philosophical terms. In this case he crosses Hegel's thinking of negativity with the language of finite sense and finite existence such as it is developed in works such as *Une Pensée finie* and *Le Sens du monde*. In this context, the language of finitude gives way to, or becomes intimately bound

---

[11] For an excellent account of this tradition see Bruce Baugh, *French Hegel* (2003).

[12] Nancy very clearly runs overturns a dominant post-war reading of Hegel which sees in dialectical thought a totalitarian tendency. Hegel, he writes, 'is not a totalitarian thinker' (Nancy 2002: 8). In this context, his concerns in this text are very different from those of his very early work *La Remarque spéculative: un bon mot de Hegel* (Nancy 1973).

up with, the language of infinity or infinitude.[13] This crossing of terms and intertwining of the language of the finite and the infinite can be seen in the very opening pages of the Hegel book when, for instance, Nancy talks about the negative in relation to the 'time' of the Hegelian subject and of the historical world:

> this is what *time* is, the concrete existence of negativity, this world which is the reign of the finite conceals and reveals within itself the infinite work of negativity, that is to say the restlessness [*l'inquiétude*] of sense (or of the 'concept' as Hegel calls it). (Nancy 2002: 5)

Here, in a careful juxtaposition of terms, Nancy aligns the 'infinite work of negativity' with 'sense' and, in turn, this 'restless' sense is aligned with the Hegelian 'concept'. Sense comes to stand in for the German *Begriff* rather than for the term *Sinn*. This, in itself, might represent a significant shift for Nancy insofar as he talks, in earlier works, about *finite* sense and does so within a context that both repeats and transforms Heidegger's thinking of *Sinn* in *Sein und Zeit*.[14] In the work on Hegel, then, sense (that is to say, the sense of the world, the sense that is or makes a world) both repeats and transforms the Hegelian 'concept' [*Begriff*] of the *Phenomenology of Spirit*, and with this becomes a figure for the infinitude of the finite.

In some ways, the reading of Hegel as a whole in *L'Inquiétude du négatif* can be seen far more as Nancy rereading *himself* in a way which uses the Hegelian 'restless' negative to 'infinitize' finitude, to transform finite thinking, and to name the nothing differently. The manner in which the finite is 'transformed' by the infinity of the negative is articulated very clearly by Nancy himself when he speaks of:

> the full and complete actuality of the infinite that traverses, works, and transforms the finite. Which means: negativity, the empty hollow [*le creux*], the gap, the difference of being which relates to itself through this very difference, and which *is* thus, in all its essence and all its energy, and thus the infinite act of relating to itself, and thus the power of the negative. (Nancy 2002: 9)

Nancy has arguably found here another language and another set of terms to name the 'nothing'. Whereas in *La Communauté désœuvrée* terms such as 'being which "is not"', 'excess', 'outside', 'rending apart' and 'clinamen' named the nothing of being-with, in the Hegel book of 1997 this nothing is named as 'negativity', 'hollow', 'gap'. Only 'the difference of being which relates to itself by that very difference' might recall the ontological difference of Heideggerian finite being, but this is a difference become infinite, an infinite act of being 'relating to itself' infinitely. In effect, Nancy's reading of Hegel

---

[13] Nancy is very careful to repeat Hegel's distinction between 'good' and 'bad' infinity. 'Bad' infinity would imply the infinity of a progression or unending expansion. 'Good' infinity is actual and, as it were, already traversing the finite; it is 'the instability of all finite determination' (Nancy 2002: 12).

[14] For an extended discussion of this see James 2006: 80–97.

allows him to re-inscribe the thinking of the nothing outside of the register of finite being and finitude. Just as he formerly took up the idiom of Heidegge-rian ontology and interweaved it with other registers and other terms, so he now takes up the idiom of Hegelian phenomenology in order again to interweave or cross different philosophical discourses. Here, the excess of finite being is rethought as a relation of infinity or as an infinite relation:

> Such is the first and fundamental signification of absolute negativity: the negative is the prefix of the *in*-finite, as the affirmation that all finitude (and every being *is* finite) is in itself in excess of its determi-nacy. It is an infinite relation [*dans le rapport infini*] (Nancy 2002: 12).[15]

This represents both a continuity and a shift in Nancy's thinking. It is a continuity insofar as he continues to develop his own thought in a gesture of taking up, reinscribing, interweaving and transforming different philosophi-cal registers and idioms. It is a shift insofar as the language of finitude finds itself subordinated to a far greater emphasis on the language of infinity. The nothing, the absolute negativity of the negative, is re-inscribed as infinity or the infinite relation of all finite existence to itself.[16]

It may be that this shift relates to an increasing concern on Nancy's part to distance himself from the language of finitude. This may itself be a response to some of the critical reception of Nancy's work, which has arguably tended to focus in too limited a way on the persistence of Heidegger in his 'finite thinking' and his ontology of the singular plural. Blanchot's reproach in *La Communauté inavouable* has, perhaps, had a long afterlife in the responses of those commentators who have been critical of Nancy's persistence with the language of ontology. It is possible that such criticisms have to some degree inflected the development of Nancy's thought. Either

---

[15] In earlier works such as *Une Penseé finie* (1990; translated as *A Finite Thinking* 2003b), Nancy has a rather negative understanding of the infinite. He cites Heidegger for example: '"When being is posited as infinite, it is precisely then that it is deter-mined. If it is posited as finite, it is then that its absence of ground is affirmed"' (Nancy 2003b: 9). Later Nancy adds: 'All that remains for us is to think this finite character [of being] as such without infinitizing it' (Nancy 2003b: 11).

[16] After the 1997 work on Hegel, Nancy's writing far more consistently invokes the infinite, the infinity of sense, of relation and of all determinate existence. This is a key aspect of his 'deconstruction of Christianity'. This shift in vocabulary has been noted by Howard Caygill (Caygill 2005). In particular, Caygill analyses the language of the infinite in Nancy's short work *Noli me tangere* (Nancy 2003c). He argues that Nancy's 'simultaneous presencing and absencing of the infinite in the finite' (Caygill 2005: 354) leads him to reject his earlier understanding of community in favour of an understanding which is closer to that of Levinas. According to Caygill, Nancy rejects his early attempt to embody community and, like Levinas, makes of it a: 'site of witness for the absent God and the joyful promise of an other fraternal community' (Caygill 2005: 356). One might want to question here both the degree to which Nancy has ever sought to 'embody' community, and the degree to which Nancy's use of the language of infinitude really entails a close alignment of his thinking with that of Levinas. The 1997 book on Hegel might suggest that Nancy is taking his own, rather singular path into the language of infinity.

way, it is clear that Nancy's thinking of community, of being-with, and of the nothing which community *is*, or to which it is exposed, is always a thinking in which ontology, in its persistence, persistently opens out beyond itself. It is always gesturing towards that which exceeds ontological naming or disclosure, it is always itself exposed to excess, outside, or the actual infinite which traverses the finite.

Nancy's philosophical writing enacts or performs this exposure of thought to its own excess in the weaving together, repetition, and transformation of a range of philosophical idioms. In this sense, his exchange with Blanchot on the question of community highlights the extent to which his thinking always needs to be read as a form of sharing or as itself a certain affirmation of community. The motif of sharing (in French the term is *partage*) persists in Nancy's thinking from the early 1980s onwards. It is a term to which Nancy returns once more in *La Communauté affrontée* to describe, once more, the 'in-common' of existence:

> There has already been between us – all of us together and through togetherness distinct – the sharing of an in-common which is only its sharing, but which in being shared makes exist and therefore touches on existence itself insofar as existence is an exposure to its own limit. It is this that makes 'us,' separating us and bringing us together, creating proximity through the distancing *between-us* – 'us' in the major indecision where this collective or plural subject is maintained, condemned never to find is own voice. (Nancy 2001: 45)

If this is a description of 'communal existence', of being-singular-plural, or being-with, it is also a very precise description of Nancy's 'community of writing' and of the 'writing of community'. Between Blanchot and Bataille, Heidegger and Hegel, between all the proper names and philosophical figures which Nancy's writing invokes and weaves together, there is a sharing of a thinking of the nothing. This emerges as an always singular and plural naming, in which nothing other than a shared exposure to an absence or withdrawal is shared. This is not a community of identity where that which is named is rendered substantial and substantially present. Rather, it is a community of writing, a writing of absence irreducible to any school and irreducible to the self-identity of a proper name or philosophical idiom.

Towards the end of *La Communauté inavouable*, Blanchot, it may be recalled, questioned whether the unavowable of community should prescribe or demand silence. Yet he immediately conceded that in order to remain silent it is necessary to speak. In this respect, it may be that the exchange between Blanchot and Nancy on the question of community, and indeed the entirety of Nancy's subsequent thinking about communal existence, need to be placed under the sign of a certain paradoxical affirmation of silence. This is a silence marked in a certain gesture of words and in an affirmation of that 'nothing' which words cannot avow or make present. To this extent, what is at stake is therefore also a silence which precedes any logic of speech or of falling silent in the traditional sense (just as the absence which has been at stake throughout this discussion precedes any logic or possibility of presence). Silence here imposes itself, or perhaps rather withdraws itself, as that radical exteriority or unspeakability, as that radical absence which makes a demand upon thought and upon the thinking of community. It is a silence to which only writing can respond. Towards the end of *L'Entretien infini* Blanchot writes:

> Writing marks but leave no trace [*L'écriture trace, mais ne laisse pas de trace*]; it does not authorize us to work our way back from some vestige or sign to anything other than itself as (pure) exteriority – never given, never gathering itself in a relation of unity with a presence (to be seen, to be heard), with the totality of presence or the Unique, present-absent. (Blanchot 1993: 426)

The unavowable of community cannot be said, but at the very same time in writing it never ceases to be marked or traced. Nancy himself puts this in the following terms: 'The unavowable never ceases to be said or to say itself in the intimate silence of those who could avow but never can avow' (Nancy 2001: 40). In between the texts written by Blanchot and Nancy, and in between the terms and philosophical idioms which are woven together to make those texts, there is the gap, the spacing, the excess which has always already withdrawn. This is a withdrawal in which a certain silence is spoken.

Towards the end of *La Communauté affrontée*, it might also be recalled, Nancy affirmed that it is the task of thought to dare to think the unthinkable of being-with without submitting it to any hypostasis (Nancy 2001: 50). The task would be to think the 'nothing' without returning it to all-powerful and all-present monstrosity (Nancy 2001: 45). At the beginning of the twenty-first century, in a globalised world rent apart by internecine conflict, there may be a need, more than ever, to think community outside of figures of totality and projects of shared destiny. In this context, both Blanchot and Nancy remind us that ethical and political stakes of thinking community in the absence of metaphysical ground are always a matter of thinking community as absence. Yet they also remind us that this thinking of community occurs in the experience of the 'community of writing'. It is only in the anonymity of writing, in its incessant restlessness and indeterminacy, that the 'nothing' of community can be spoken in the very moment of its withdrawal into intimate silence.

References

Baugh, B. 2003. *French Hegel*. London: Routledge.

Blanchot, M. 1983. *La Communauté inavouable*. Paris: Minuit.

Blanchot, M. 1988. *The Unavowable Community*. Translated by P. Joris. New York: Station Hill Press.

Blanchot, M. 1993. *The Infinite Conversation*. Translated by S. Hanson. Minneapolis, MN: University of Minnesota.

Caygill, H. 2005. 'Bearing Witness to the Infinite: Nancy and Levinas'. *Journal for Cultural Research* 9:4, 351–57.

Critchley, S. 1993. 'Retracing the Political: Politics and Community in the Works of Lacoue-Labarthe and Jean-Luc Nancy'. In D. Campbell & M. Dillon (eds), *The Political Subject of Violence*. Manchester: Manchester University Press, 73–93.

Derrida, J. 2000. *Jacques Derrida, Le Toucher: Jean-Luc Nancy*. Paris: Galilée.

Derrida, J. 2003. *Voyous*. Paris: Galilée.

Derrida, J. 2005a. *On Touching – Jean-Luc Nancy*. Translated by C. Irizarry. Stanford, CA: Stanford University Press.

Derrida, J. 2005b. *Rogues*. Translated by P.-A. Brault & M. Naas. Stanford, CA: Stanford University Press.

Fraser, N. 1984. 'The French Derrideans: Politicizing Deconstruction or Deconstructing the Political?'. *New German Critique* 33, 127–54.

Gaon, S. 2005. 'Communities in Question: Sociality and Solidarity in Nancy and Blanchot'. *Journal for Cultural Research* 9:4, 387–403.

Hill, L. 1996. *Maurice Blanchot Extreme Contemporary*. London: Routledge.

Huntingdon, S. P. 1996 *The Clash of Civilizations and the Remaking of World Order*. New York: Simon & Schuster.

Ingram, D. 1988. 'The Retreat from the Political in the Modern Age: Jean-Luc Nancy on Totalitarianism and Community'. *Research in Phenomenology* 18, 93–124.

James, I. 2005. 'On Interrupted Myth'. *Journal for Cultural Research* 9:4, 331–49.

James, I. 2006. *The Fragmentary Demand: An Introduction to the Philosophy of Jean-Luc Nancy*. Stanford, CA: University of Stanford Press.

Nancy, J.-L. 1973. *La Remarque spéculative: un bon mot de Hegel*. Paris: Galilée.

Nancy, J.-L. 1983. 'La Communauté désœuvrée'. *Aléa* 4, 11–49

Nancy, J.-L. 1985. *La Communauté désœuvrée*. Paris: Christian Bourgois.

Nancy, J.-L. 1988. *L'Expérience de la liberté*. Paris: Galilée.

Nancy, J.-L. 1990. *Une pensée finie*. Paris: Galilée.

Nancy, J.-L. 1991a. *The Inoperative Community*. Translated by P. Connor et al. Minneapolis, MN: University of Minnesota Press.

Nancy, J.-L. 1991b. *La Comparution*. Paris: Christian Bourgois.

Nancy, J.-L. 1993a. *Le Sens du monde*. Paris: Galilée.

Nancy, J.-L. 1993b. *The Experience of Freedom*. Translated by B. McDonald. Stanford, CA: Stanford University Press.

Nancy, J.-L. 1997a. *The Gravity of Thought*. Translated by F. Raffoul & G. Rocco. Atlantic Highlands: Humanities Press.

Nancy, J.-L. 1997b. *Être singulier pluriel*. Paris: Galilée.

Nancy, J.-L. 1997c. *The Sense of the World*. Translated by J. S. Librett. Minneapolis, MN: University of Minnesota Press.

Nancy, J.-L. 1997d. *Hegel: L'Inquiétude du negative*. Paris: Hachette.

Nancy, J.-L. 2000. *Being Singular Plural*. Translated by A. E. O'Byrne & R. D. Richardson. Stanford, CA: Stanford University Press.

Nancy, J.-L. 2001. *La Communauté affrontée*. Paris: Galilée.

Nancy, J.-L. 2002. *Hegel: The Restlessness of the Negative*. Translated by J. Smith & S. Miller. Minneapolis, MN: University of Minnesota Press.

Nancy, J.-L. 2003a. 'The Confronted Community'. *Postcolonial Studies* 9:4, 23–36.

Nancy, J.-L. 2003b. *A Finite Thinking*. Translated by S. Sparks. Stanford, CA: Stanford University Press.

Nancy, J.-L. 2003c. *Noli me tangere*. Paris: Bayard.

Nancy, J.-L. & P. Lacoue-Labarthe. 1983. *Le Retrait du Politique*. Paris: Gallimard.

Nancy, J.-L. & P. Lacoue-Labarthe. 1997. *Retreating the Political*. Translated by C. Surprenant, R. Stamp, L. Hill et al. London: Routledge.

Norris, A. 2000. 'Jean-Luc Nancy and the Myth of the Common'. *Constellations* 9:4, 272–95.

Readings, B. 1989. 'The Deconstruction of Politics'. In L. Waters & W. Godzich (eds), *De Man Reading de Man*. Minneapolis, MN: University of Minnesota Press, 223–43.

Next to Nothing: Jean Paulhan's Gamble

Anna-Louise Milne

Abstract   *Articulating together Jean Paulhan's texts on language, painting and the experience of the Resistance during the Nazi Occupation of France, this article distinguishes between the nothingness or silence that is one face of a totalising opposition – between signs and things – and the 'small nothings' that recur throughout Paulhan's texts. It argues that these 'nothings,' odd snippets and scraps of a culture that are overlooked or dismissed rather than reduced to nothing by the priorities of power, offer the possibility of restoring a sense of community when a polity ceases to speak a common language, as arguably occurred in France during the Occupation. Thus it dismisses the claim that Paulhan's work was essentially apolitical, and challenges the deconstructive approach that concludes on its aporetic nature. In contrast, it concludes that Paulhan offers a vital reflection on the power of words to ground a common purpose.*

In 1941, Jean Paulhan ended his long-awaited critical essay, *Les Fleurs de Tarbes*, with the retraction: 'let's say I said nothing' (Paulhan 1990: 168). In February 1944, he equated nothingness with the Nazi Occupation in his short piece 'L'abeille', in which he set the tone for his version of the motivations underpinning the decision to enter into resistance, which would later lead him into conflict with his comrades when the times turned to purges. In this latter piece, he contrasts the nothingness that the Nazis spread around them with 'small nothings' that are what prompt action and sustain life:

> If we had been occupied (as we say politely) by the Swedes, we would at least be left with a dance step, a taste for blue and yellow ribbons; by the Javanese, a particular way of twiddling one's fingers; by the Hottentots, the Italians, the Hungarians, we would be left with a song, a smile, a little nod of the head. In short, one of those absurd mannerisms that don't mean anything precise – that signify simply that we're happy to be alive, that we prefer that to not living at all, that it is amusing (in particular) to have a body, source of all sorts of fantastical possibilities. But from them, we can all see that nothing

will be left. Not a song, not a grimace … They will have passed like a great emptiness. (Paulhan 1970b: 287)[1]

In the following discussion I want to tease out what is at stake between this death-like nothingness and the life-sustaining nothings, and take that distinction back to the retraction at the end of *Les Fleurs de Tarbes*, an apparent critical aporia that has been influentially read as a precursor to deconstructive thinking. My aim is to explore another mode of reading it, which opens on to a specific political challenge.

Paulhan is difficult to place in intellectual history. Schooled in empirical psychology, he did a stint as a teacher in Madagascar, from 1908 to 1910, where he became fascinated with Malagasy proverbs and developed an interest in early ethnography, much informed by the dominant comparative approaches to linguistics of the time. On his return to France, he signed up to do a PhD with one of the eminent ethnographers of the day, Lucien Levy-Bruhl, and one of Saussure's most influential pupils, Antoine Meillet. However, he also gravitated towards the surrealist movement and, after the war, during which he was injured seriously with a head wound, he wrote a number of *récits* characterised by marked formal experimentation. To a certain extent, this combination of a proclivity for poetic exploration and a determination to achieve institutional recognition – he continued to work towards his PhD project for over ten years – came together in Paulhan's appointment as editor of the increasingly prominent *La Nouvelle Revue Française*, a relatively mainstream literary monthly which gained such widespread influence throughout the 1930s that the joke was, on the eve of the Occupation, that there were three key areas that Nazis had to control to subjugate France: the banks, the Communist Party and *La Nouvelle Revue Française*.

Paulhan's long interwar career at the *NRF* – from 1925 to 1940, when the publication was indeed taken over by the occupying forces and Paulhan resigned – was not, however, merely a gradual consolidation of a position of establishment influence. While *La Nouvelle Revue Française* was perceived as the bastion of a certain idea of literary purity, Paulhan was involved in all number of other enterprises, from the *Collège de sociologie*, to municipal politics during the Popular Front, as well as working on his own texts which, in many respects, challenge the orientation of the journal he steered so expertly to pre-eminence. To complete the short summary of this eclectic career, he entered into active resistance very early in 1940, headed up one of the most influential resistance publications, then spoke out, again very early, against the literary purges – the *épuration*, as it was known – in the wake of the war, ostracising himself from a large swathe of the new literary establishment. In the meantime, his work had moved from primarily language and literary issues to a focus on painting, and particularly cubist painting, which, by the 1940s, was somewhat old news. All of which provides a difficult series of choices to make sense of, and some commentators have indeed concluded that both as a body of work and a lifetime achievement, ultimately it does not

---

[1] All translations of Paulhan's works cited herein are mine

hold together, and that his intention was always more that of the trickster, impossible to pin down.

In contrast, the reading that will be elaborated here begins with a strong sense of the architectural ambition of Paulhan's work, which is materialised in the form of countless plans and diagrams sketching how small sections of writing would coalesce to form a full volume.[2] These plans show a tendency to return to specific examples and short accounts of events, despite an apparently different focus to the overall project. Thus, sections of the unfinished thesis find their way into post-war essays on Rhetoric; the 'aventure en pleine nuit' section of the essay on cubism quoted below plays an important role in the later exploration of mystical thinking entitled *Le Clair et l'obscur*; and examples invoked in his pre-1914 articles re-surface in his notes from the 1950s. This tendency undoubtedly diminishes the impact of contemporary thinkers on his work. Indeed, his engagement with the massive presence of Sartre is exemplary of his, at times, extremely reductive method which enables him to re-articulate his own central preoccupations. His 1950 contribution to *La Table Ronde*, entitled 'Jean-Paul Sartre n'est pas en bons termes avec les mots' ['*Jean-Paul Sartre is not on good terms with words*'] focuses exclusively on Sartre's critical essays and identifies the same tendency to confuse signs as signifiers – mere words cut from thoughts, in Paulhan's formulation – with signs as signifieds that had structured his thinking on proverbs in the 1920s and informed his preparatory articles for *Les Fleurs de Tarbes* throughout the 1930s.[3] Paulhan was undoubtedly impressed by Sartre's pre-war fiction, to the point perhaps of re-thinking his *Fleurs de Tarbes* project entirely between 1936 and the second version in 1941 in light of *La Nausée*, but, by the end of the war, political differences (discussed in more detail below) muddied any possibility for Paulhan of sustained engagement with the evolving concepts of existentialism. He did join the editorial board of *Les Temps modernes* at its inception, although privately expressing his reservations to André Gide about the journal's orientation:

> Sartre has just written a manifesto for *Les Temps modernes* (ex-*Condition humaine*). Its Marxist component seems quite solid, and its

---

[2] These plans and notes are held in the vast Paulhan archives at the Institut memoires de l'édition contemporaine at the Abbaye d'Ardenne. They provide important insight into the palimpsest method that Paulhan favoured, often cutting out and gluing early sections of manuscript of printed work into new projects. The metaphors of architecture and sketching acquire their resonance in the light of these archives too, for we realise the extent of Paulhan's attention to the composing on his text on the page.

[3] See *Correspondance Paulhan-Belaval* for a fascinating exchange of letters between a university professor of philosophy, specialist of Leibniz and Diderot, and Paulhan, who remains impervious to the critiques and pointers offered by his respectful but unforgiving reader (Paulhan 2004: 92–145). Belaval also lends Paulhan a copy of Merleau-Ponty's *Phenomenology of Perception* in 1948 in response to a request for some guidance on what to read to understand 'language without words.' On returning the book, Paulhan writes: 'I am returning the Merleau-Ponty. Thank you. It is nice [*gentil*] and troubling [*consternant*]'. His interest in the philosopher appears to have stopped there, and evidence in his writings shows that he returns to his original frame of reference, in this instance the Enlightenment philosopher Maine de Biran (1766–1824) (Paulhan 2004: 83).

metaphysical component totally chimerical. Flaubert was wrong not to condemn the Commune, Proust to write about heterosexual love. So be it, and long live engaged literature, as we say! But Sartre can only get himself out of a Marxist frame by spinning on a notion of human freedom one hundred times lighter than Albertine. (I have agreed to join the editorial board, which I don't see how it can avoid being anything but boring and false. But in literature everything has its use [*en littérature tout sert*]. (Paulhan 1992: 391)

He nonetheless resigned very quickly, and subsequently his marginalisation within contemporary debate grew with the increasingly fractious political climate, a marginalisation that has undoubtedly conditioned reception of Paulhan's work even into the late twentieth century. Indeed, the unlikely yoking together of wildly disparate discourses and practices – from Malagasy proverbs to Cubist collages – across a long period of reflection has prevented commentators from discerning how his thinking consolidates over time, while his explicit mistrust of political institutions and parties has made it all too easy to relegate him to a reactionary camp. Whether in the face of his incomprehension when close friends and mentors – from André Gide to Francis Ponge – threw their lot in with the Communist Party, or when other close friends – Marcel Jouhandeau, for example – gravitated towards proto-fascism and eventually collaboration, historians have tended to perceive a form of conservative apoliticism. This reading of his apoliticism fails, however, to allow for a deeper-seated preoccupation with what underpins the parameters of political discourse, and it is at this level that I want to focus here on how 'nothing' or, rather, the 'nothings' which fall outside what we can or do say, have, by this very fact, the potential to change the grammar of our lives.

I will turn primarily to the major text Paulhan finished after the war, *La Peinture cubiste*, to expand on the 'nothings' that he invokes in the short piece 'L'abeille', quoted above. This analysis will then enable us to read the retraction at the end of *Les Fleurs de Tarbes* in a broader light that sets Paulhan's assertion 'let's say I said nothing' apart from the sort of undecidability that challenges the sovereignty of a discursive field. Indeed, my point will be to stress that this assertion paradoxically reaffirms the sovereignty of certain words and their power to give form to our shared lives. First, however, I want to come back to why political institutions are given such short shrift, implicitly in the 'L'abeille' text, as in all of the short texts that Paulhan published in the wake of the war, and explicitly throughout his copious correspondence. This will enable us to appreciate better what sort of political act can be construed from his writings.

Rewriting the past

The 'little nothings' of the gestures and ribbons, songs and smiles, are not only what would have lasted on beyond another sort of occupation, an occupation that had worked its way into the fabric of life, rather than just spreading death around it, as he says of the Nazi occupation. They are also the reason why people entered into resistance activities. Most accounts of Paulhan's decision to resign from the post-Resistance National Committee of Writers (CNE), when they issued a black list of authors who had collaborated and with whom they now refused all association, have focused on his claim that writers should be entitled to a 'right to error' because they are writers and, therefore, in some sense, engaged only on the plane of fabulation and fiction, indifferent to the purchase their words have in the real world. Paulhan did indeed invoke a 'right to error', but his justification for this claim had nothing to do with writing being divorced from action. On the contrary, it was informed by a conception of the future as fully open and unpredictable, and of writers as those people who experience most intimately that openness, with the risks entailed by suspending all assurance that patterns of meaning will continue to obtain.

Thus, he repeatedly rejected the *ex post facto* accounts of Resistance activities that underscored the sense of destiny, of fighting for an unquestionably good cause. In 'L'abeille', written in February 1944, he claims first that even those firmly on the now evidently victorious side of the Allies had a vague sense of solidarity with Vichy, despite thinking the collaborators to be 'bastards'. For Paulhan, it was of paramount importance to remain alive to the difficulty of reading the events that had surrounded the emergence of the Resistance, that is to avoid re-writing the past. Contrary to a dominant universalist discourse that Gisèle Shapiro has so well-documented in her study of French writers through the war, he articulated an understanding of these events that modelled certain individuals running certain risks for reasons they only vaguely understood at the time and which they had certainly not consolidated in a system of belief in advance of acting (Shapiro 1999: 571–81). Doubt, recklessness, intuition were all part of the picture, and they only made those who did decide to resist all the more 'heroic' for their commitment was made without 'necessity'. Moreover, Paulhan also insists that the effects of this decision were inadequate to sustain conviction. The point is to insist on the *free* nature of the decision to enter into resistance, to divorce it from any notion of rationale. Thus, he answers the criticism that those who opposed the occupier often died for very little measurable effect by arguing that they died for precisely the same insignificant things that would have been bequeathed by a 'life-sustaining' occupying army:

> I know what they say – that they died for not much. A snippet of information (and not always very reliable information) did not justify that, nor a tract, nor even an underground newspaper (which was often rather poorly put together). To those detractors, we have to answer: 'They were on the side of life. They liked quite insignificant things: a song, a snap of the fingers, a smile.' You can squeeze a bee in your hand until it suffocates. It won't suffocate without first stinging you. That's not much, you say. No, not much. But if the bee didn't sting you, it would be a long time since there had been any bees. (Paulhan 1970b: 288)

In his later and much maligned text, *Lettre aux Directeurs de la Résistance*, he adds to this vision of the lightly-held decision to join the Resistance a further apparent affront to that heroic history: those who did take that decision were only at the beginning of their resistance; it was a decision that needed to be renewed every day, and most terribly in the face of torture. The resistance fighter was not forever on the side of right, relieved of one's need to weigh the consequences of action by belief in the enemy's evil. Rather, he or she was constantly in danger of becoming a 'bastard' by betraying that decision: 'Thus the first decision led to other decisions (far more serious ones). The initial burst of courage led to further bursts of courage (much more heroic ones). Far from being right for the rest of life, they were always at risk of being unjust, of becoming, from one day to the next, a bastard' (Paulhan 1987: 7–9). In this respect – in the sense of choosing to engage outside the boundaries of 'legally' sanctioned behaviour – Paulhan in fact establishes an equation between the writer and the resistance fighter. Both have suspended their hold on language: speaking becomes a minefield for anyone engaged in clandestine activities for words acquire consequences none can predict, just as they potentially do for the sort of writer Paulhan was interested in – the sort of writer who challenged the self-consistency of language.

The postwar purges were the moment when Paulhan's writings came closest to the political fray: reactive, written quickly, they stand apart from his much more crafted essays that were generally years in the making. But they are not anomalies. Rather, they bear the trace of the momentary instability of language as a new discursive regime found its mark after the silence, or death, spread by the 'nothingness' of the Nazi occupation. Propelled by the victory of the Allies out of a state in which what was most 'between' people was precisely what could not be said officially, out loud and for general dissemination, Paulhan perceives the speed with which national discourse was re-congealing around certain 'truths'. In December 1944, in another of his short polemical pieces, he declares: 'It's crazy how we find ourselves wanting an underground newspaper in recent times … The thing is, the ordinary newspapers – the ones you buy in the newsagents, the ones that are not underground – are too much alike' (Paulhan 1970a: 300). Indirectly, allusively, by teasing and prompting, his aim is to stem the consolidation of a post-Resistance orthodoxy. This meant refusing to take position substantially, offering almost flippant gestures to counter the seriousness with which a new regime of truth was establishing itself. In this respect, his rhetorical manoeuvres appear both predictable, perhaps even pedantic, and at the same time facile or irrelevant. On the one hand, he attempts to normalise what is unanimously perceived as an exceptional situation, yet, on the other, as we have seen, he makes an apparently disproportionate investment in odd expressions and events, which appear intimately but inconsequentially tied to the moment. And this combination left not only his contemporaries bewildered, but has continued to leave historians nonplussed.[4]

---

[4] Most notably Jeannine Verdès-Leroux expresses her confusion in terms that barely disguise her disgust at Paulhan's apparent flippancy: 'Today these texts seem to me to be neither iconoclastic nor stimulating. Rather they are nothing much more than a not very funny game. Copying out old reflections from Aragon – "what repels us is the idea of a homeland, which is really the most bestial concept", "my country, which I detest, where everything that is French provokes a sense of revolt in me to that extent that it is *French*" (1925) – seems like a very weak joke. What did Paulhan think he could achieve? Did he want to save some friends? To reveal the villainous nature of others?' (1996: 407–8).

This duality corresponds, however, to the give between nothingness and nothings, which I signalled at the beginning. Throughout his writings, Paulhan returns insistently to a logic of language in which emptiness or silence are figured as the reverse face of action and impulse, thus setting up analogies that do make his work seem at times overly constricted, indifferent to the charge of the present moment. Yet this logic tends to be narrativised in ways that destabilise it. For example, at the end of the text 'Les Morts', he repeats but transforms the logical claim that all language is undercut by what it excludes – by what it silences – with an evocation of the silence of those who gave their lives to resistance. Their silence is both what post-Resistance patriotism can no longer hear, or say, if it is to become the new language of political power, and the irrepressibility of idiomatic speech, which rings through in the almost colloquial nature of the expression 'ceux qui se sont tus' (Paulhan 1970a: 302), signifying both a decision to fall silent and death.

The first thing we need to observe about 'openness' in this expression – which, I want to suggest, is also the openness between one mode of silence during the Occupation and another that comes with the lionising of the Resistance – is the combination of overdetermination and underdetermination at play. This is another way of configuring the give between nothingness and nothings. Having underscored the death-like propensity of the Nazi Occupation, Paulhan gently extends an analogy between this emptiness and the regime that is consolidating its power in the wake of victory. He does not run shy of the evident disproportion involved in claiming that both spread silence or death around them as a consequence of their monopoly on 'truth'. In Lettre aux Directeurs de la Résistance, this analogy becomes explicit in the final twist of his argument quoted above that Resistance was not a state of grace, entered into once and for all: 'I take the liberty of saying that they have fallen into the trap: no less cowardly and treacherous, no less unjust than those amongst them who, on the torture table, grassed on their comrades. (But with fewer excuses)' (Paulhan 1987: 9). Likewise, Paulhan presses the idea of a formal equivalence between someone like Aragon's pre-war 'collaboration' with Soviet Russia and wartime collaboration with Germany. Despite their unlikeliness, these equivalences in fact rehearse the main thrust of all Paulhan's pre-1940 work, exemplifying what he argued to be a systematic feature of discursive organisation. Most often this argument took the form of a discussion of the word/idea opposition, which corresponds more or less to Saussure's signifier/signified distinction, with which Paulhan was familiar. Proverbs were the first phenomena around which he articulated his observation that some speakers perceive these expressions as mere empty words against the contrary observation that they have the power to move people to action. Henceforth, his thinking worked out of the idea that every mere word is also a consequential thought. Thus, language in the broadest sense, for Paulhan, is inscribed upon both its capacity to negate itself by making the thing or idea immediately present to the mind, and its power to empty the world of 'things' by drawing attention only to its 'wordiness'.

The notion of a 'commonplace', which is the primary focus of his most influential work Les Fleurs de Tarbes, captures this bivalency most succinctly for him, being synonymous with both the 'dead words' of a cliché and with the rich expressive possibilities of the classical 'topos.' And, in the first version of this essay published in 1936, he insists on the absolute mutually excluding nature of these two visions, for one reduces the other to nothingness:

> In a period of rhetoric, *commonplace* refers to a general idea, argument, or proof – whatever is most abstract, like a pure vector of thought. In a period of terror, it refers to a stereotyped or mechanical sentence, that is, whatever in the sentence is most material. The latter is a word that has fled any idea, the former an idea that escapes words. Far from them coinciding, I cannot see how, from one to the other, there could even be a passage or a bridge, if there is nothing of the word – noise, sound, sign, writing – that falls in naturally with the meanings [*ne tombe sous les sens*], but nothing of the meaning that escapes them. (Paulhan 1990: 246)

In the first version of the essay, he moves from this hiatus between unreflective immersion within a discursive order and incomprehending exclusion from it, to the projection of a series of visual models that might enable a glimpse of the passage from one to the other. In the later version, to put things simply, he replaces these visual models with the retraction I quoted above. That assertion of nothingness thus subvenes in the place of the hiatus. But before really getting on to what that assertion, which is also a retraction, makes possible, we need to stay a little longer with the hiatus. It is the key to Paulhan's increasing engagement with political commentary in the latter half of the 1930s.

In 1938, he began a polemical exchange with the editors of the journal *Les Nouveaux Cahiers*, criticising their regular column that aimed to awaken readers to the dangers of adopting words such as 'democracy', 'fascism', 'classes', 'terrorism' as creeds. As Paulhan points out, *Les Nouveaux Cahiers* was only repeating a rhetorical gesture inscribed in political discourse since the Revolution. The absence of an absolute authority, previously embodied in the monarch, leaves language open to endless contestation and slippage, even to the extent that, in periods of Terror, words can come to signify their opposite, 'political representation' to mean 'dictatorship', 'fascism' to mean 'division' and 'annihilation', 'democracy' to mean 'occupation' and 'subjugation'. And what he objected to in the approach of *Les Nouveaux Cahiers* was the implication that these discrepancies could and should be dispelled by making language signify correctly and consistently. In contrast, he argued forcefully, from his perception of a hiatus between two modes of reception of given words, that 'mere' expressions cannot possibly exercise power, for if they are perceived precisely as 'mere' expressions or chimeras, then they are devoid of purchase. Whereas if people are moved to action, then their reception of the 'words' compelling them to this action is of anything but 'mere' words: 'In truth, there is something violently absurd in wanting to imagine such a power of words. For the simplest experience tells us that where there is power, words are invisible; and where words are apparent, there is no more power' (Paulhan 1990: 104).

In some respects, the position Paulhan takes here is comparable to Judith Butler's work on hate speech. She focuses on how certain speech acts – racist slander and pornography in particular – can replace the absent monarch as a means of unifying the field of power, thus allowing the belief that political action depends on legislating against these elements of speech. And she brings to the fore the key assumption underpinning this sort of legislation, which is that there is a stable relation between intention and action, or words and their effects. She shows that focusing on the power of words to wound, or to foster sentiments of rage or solidarity, casts the speaking subject in the role of violator which, in turn, invites the belief that injury or violation can be prevented by disciplining those subjects who use this 'performative' language:

> By locating the cause of our injury in a speaking subject and the power of that injury in the power of speech, we set ourselves free, as it were, to seek recourse to the law – now set against power and imagined as neutral – in order to control that onslaught of hateful words. (Butler 1997: 80)

Butler's attention is to the supposed neutrality of the law, while Paulhan's is to the apparent neutrality of some language in contrast to the 'agitation' or 'influence' of certain expressions. This difference is significant because Paulhan has to be read in another light to that of post-Marxist philosophy such as that of Foucault, whose work is a crucial reference for Butler. His focus remains on the individual, or groups of individuals, and more importantly, in contrast to anti-individualist theories of the subject, he repeatedly underscored the difficulty of making meaning – of 'accomplishing' it – which inevitably puts society always at the edge of splintering into mutually incomprehending factions. Paulhan and Butler share a suspicion of the tendency to reduce politics to a question of language use for they see how this ignores the slippage between how words are used and how they are received, but where Butler concentrates on the possibilities for re-negotiation around certain utterances, which might shift the hold of language on us, Paulhan explores a more spontaneous and transformative event that opens up the perspective of universal accord. The key characteristic of this event is its underdetermination.

Shaping the future

In addition to making provocative jibes at the rationalisation of post-Liberation discourse, Paulhan also began at this time to work on his essay on cubism – which he would not actually begin to publish for another ten years. The switch from text to painting has fuelled a critical tendency to argue that Paulhan reversed his apparent commitment in *Les Fleurs de Tarbes* to Rhetoric and classical values by taking up the cause of avant-garde ambitions for abstract art, as if he had found some bedrock truth in painting that had eluded him in language. This reading, however, allows no account to be made of why there is this particular focus on cubist collages which were a relatively limited feature in Picasso and Braque's output and dated back essentially to 1912. In contrast, I want to suggest that his fascination with cubism had nothing to do with the way it flattened traditional, perspectival painting. Indeed, he hints in several places in his writings on art that cubism merely replaced one mode of artifice with another, in the same way that he identified two main 'regimes', or modes of 'artifice' in language, one that sees only the signified, and one the signifier. Moreover, he insists on something like the depth of these collages, and this configuration of depth or 'relief' will be important for the way he gives body to what lies in the hiatus between regimes.

Rather than a bedrock truth, then, what drew Paulhan to these collages or *papiers collés* is their unlikeliness, in 1945 and in 1912, the violence of the reactions they provoked in 1912, and the relative indifference to them in 1945. They came from nowhere in 1912, and his return to them is also, I want to argue, self-consciously intended to appear irrelevant; they subsumed everything for a while, then they subsided into relative obscurity:

> Most people – and there are plenty of them! – alive today are far too young to know what happened in painting between 1905 and 1913. At best they can only imagine a weak version of events, relying on documents that come down to us from those curious bygone days. (Paulhan 1970c: 62)

The event at issue here is, for Paulhan, the discovery of a new space – a new dimensionality. The moment of the collages, he contends, was one of openness, when no-one knew what would happen next, nor how to return back to where they had come from. In this sense, he is setting up an implicit analogy between the moment of decision to enter into the Resistance and the radical shift in aesthetic practice that provoked people to the unpredictable decision to move to Paris, or elsewhere, to throw out their previous work, to reverse the priorities of their artistic training, all without understanding fully what moved them to this. He refers to this transformation as equivalent to a religious conversion, and he insists that while it is 'fair game' to criticise those who reject abstraction, it is not legitimate to accuse them of being 'imbeciles who understand nothing about nothing'. For grasping abstraction is no longer a question of understanding, but rather of a 'parti pris' or a 'leap' (Paulhan 1970c: 72).

Equally important to the failure to appreciate what this revolution was about was the scale of what was called into doubt by it. Common to the 'blind' rejection of cubism and the 'blind' acceptance of it was the intuition that it threatened the very order of things. Paulhan retrieves a succession of panicked remarks that peppered the press at the time, calling for respect for the natural world travestied by these representations, or doubting one's very own existence as a result of confronting these visions of the human body, or calling for war in the hope that it will wipe these aberrations from the surface of the earth. All in all, what cubist collages provided him with, in those fraught post-Liberation days, was the combination of a triviality of means and an explosion of hyperbole: a revolution that hung on almost nothing – an under-conceptualised manipulation of paper – and a rhetorical reaction that displayed its own emptiness in its excess. In other words, next to nothing that showed up the nothingness of a particular discourse on the inviolable principles of art, nature and existence.

But cubism was not only, for Paulhan, another rub between the insignificant nothings that are on the side of life, pleasure, creativity, newness, and the silencing onslaught of powerful rhetoric. His essay turns around a narrative section entitled 'Petite aventure en pleine nuit', which relates something of a formative experience that resonates throughout Paulhan's post-war work. In it, he recounts the experience of returning home late to his large studio apartment where his wife is already asleep. In order not to disturb her, he flicks the light on and off extremely quickly, then proceeds on the basis of this split-second impression to make his way across the floor to their bed in the darkness. Once safely in bed, he likens the experience to a modern painting: 'I had crossed the space of a modern painting. I had in fact entered a canvas by Braque or Picasso (and I had just come out of it)' (Paulhan 1970c: 78). He makes this comparison because his experience of the room has been reduced to the meaningless 'here and now' of material inscription, to a few fragments grasped as he stumbles across the room. The 'signs' of space (the old wardrobe previously associated with the stability of perspectival or 'moral' order) and time (the ancient glass-encased clock, symbol of storytelling since it prompts a digression of the various efforts necessary to get it to work) have lost their phenomenal form and present themselves to him as 'precise and memorable figures' of the same geometrical simplicity as the famous cube of cubist paintings. And this prompts Paulhan to cite Paul Claudel's judgment that Braque and Picasso are painters of 'enseignes', shop signs or advertising. The characteristic of these signs is that they are often completely unmotivated, with no apparent relation between the image and the product or service they draw attention to. All they indicate, according to Paulhan, is the *presence* of something: a mere, but unmistakable 'there is' (Paulhan 1970c: 80). Michael Syrotinski has offered a valuable reading of this passage in terms of the materiality of the signifier, where the formal repetition of traces or sensuousness of language pushes the expository content to the background, thus disrupting the capacity of language to signify (Syrotinski 1998: 141–48). I want here to move beyond this disruptive presence to its constructive potential by following Paulhan closely as he adds that, beyond the room becoming a collection of arbitrary signs, there was 'something else' too, which he finds difficult to say:

> It was no longer a question of coming and going in my room as an amateur, for the pleasure of it. The table, the typewriter, the bricks, and the wardrobe had moved into my place, had come to the forefront. Objects were taking priority; all I could do was get used to them. These arbitrary, triumphant objects – characterized by the self-evidence of an emblem, present in the same way that a cry can be present, or a call, or a shop-sign. And precious in the same way that, for the victim of a shipwreck, a saw and a hammer saved from the wreck are precious. As mediocre and broken as they may be, they are sacred. (Paulhan 1970c: 79)

Thus, the world gets reduced to scraps by modern painting, but these scraps do more than perform their own materiality. They have personality and depth and usefulness. Moreover, the subject becomes indistinguishable from them. He can no longer come and go in the space; it no longer frames his presence but, rather, jostles alongside him, next to him:

> None of those distant places and those nearby places! Here everything was at my side [*tout m'était voisin*] ... Everything concerned me, everything was of passionate interest to me, everything was devilishly true to me. Nor any of those gently stepped visual fields, disappearing softly into the distance. Here everything was imminent, bristling with spikes, hollowed out with craters, riddled with flaws and rents! ... I was not contemplating the space of my studio. It was no longer enough for me to have an idea of it ... I had fallen into it. I found myself caught in it. I was realizing it [*Je le réalisais*], as they say ... I adhered to it (with a sort of enthusiasm or sacred intoxication). It was the opposite of a dream; it was the opposite of a thought. Not one of those fluid spaces that grow gradually deeper. No, it was perfectly opaque and voluminous; and I was no less voluminous, no less opaque. Of exactly the same race. Caught in the same aspic. (Paulhan 1970c: 79)

This passage echoes a slightly earlier one in the same essay in which Paulhan first likens the formal qualities of space to a rhetoric, insisting on the arbitrariness of the way in which volume is figured, before reclaiming an experience of space as a medium of freedom and community. Referring to this space, he enigmatically claims that within it 'the objects hold together and hold to us, and they in some way prolong us who participate in their community'. It is not possible here to explore fully the way Paulhan draws parallels between rules of linguistic expression and modes of artistic representation. I can merely draw out this notion of a 'deep' continuity between the human subject and the object world which he implies precedes or underpins any epistemological structure. He is gesturing towards a collapse of the distinction between mind and matter, which he describes elsewhere as a state of indifference, but also, and crucially, of action:

> It is part of the event, even its principal feature, that *my* thinking and *my* ideas, right up to the very vision that *I* have of things and, of course, the description that *I* sketch of that vision, have nothing to do with it. The event erases my thinking. It does not exist – if I can put it this way – to the extent that I imagine it. Rather it exists to the extent that I can't quite manage to imagine it. It escapes all ideas I represent to myself [*il échappe aux idées que je me fais*]. As if there were some adventures of the mind in which one can be only the actor, not the spectator – adventures of a secret nature, such that our attention is good only for disturbing them. (Paulhan 1970c: 82)

When Paulhan returns to his discussion of painting after this nocturnal adventure, he insists on the same continuity between spectator and painting that he has experienced with the objects in his studio. He likens the artist to an illusionist, allowing again for the arbitrary tricks that provoke an illusion of depth, but only once again to underscore the discovery of new horizons in the strange, mobile experience of space which, he stresses, is 'all the more ours in that we can use it in all senses [*que nous disposons de lui*] – in that we have entered it' (Paulhan 1970c: 133). Entering into the painting is the 'leap' referred to above, the incomprehending decision to engage with something without 'seeing' it, just as he was intimately bound up with the objects in his studio without being able to 'observe' or place them. There is no prior knowledge that can prepare one for the experience of the revolution in space brought about by cubism. This is what Paulhan was getting at with his repeated references to the colloquial expression '*on n'a pas idée de ça*' – which translates in any number of ways: 'never seen the like of it' or 'never would have thought it' – but at the loss of the implication in the original expression that this experience is prior to ideas and their counterparts: words. This idiomatic expression points back to the end of the early version of *Les Fleurs de Tarbes* where Paulhan is attempting to conceptualise the passage between two 'regimes' of perception of the commonplace, one which sees it as wordy or empty of meaning, the other as generative of meaning. He writes that the commonplace is that which presents to us 'in a state of purity – only, however, on the condition that we do not think about it too much – *that* which will later be, according to our choice, language or thought' (Paulhan 1990: 255). This experience – the experience of '*ça*' – breaks with any preceding norms, and in the process it creates the norms by which it asks to be considered. It does not collapse artifice, even though it does collapse perspective, and it is not the truth of the world. Rather it introduces a novel fantasy, which renews the viewer's contact with the world.

Paulhan formulates this apparently paradoxical idea by means of another of his allegories, this time about an explorer who writes that you can get a fairly good idea of what a rhinoceros is if you have seen a unicorn. The fantasy of the unicorn is the means to knowledge of the real. But what sort of knowledge can this be? Certainly not any that is based on experience. It can only be the world you gain by acting on the fantasy, by plunging into it and accepting it. In other words, it is the decision to hold something to be true; or, in the case of cubist collages, to decide that these constructions are 'universal':

> You have to take the oath and make the leap ... And it is the echo of this oath that has prompted good and heroic youths from around the world to rise up. Juan Gris used to say of mandolins that they were 'Braque's madonnas'. He did not know how true his words were. (Paulhan 1970c: 144)

What makes this new vision of the world 'true' is nothing more than that it prompts assent from others. Its necessity consists only in the fact that people – potentially all people – move according to it and come to define themselves in terms of it. Faced with the disenchantment of the world and the prospect of losing every means of making sense of experience – a prospect that cubist collages with their relentless reduction of painting to scraps of consumer culture make all too present – there is an urgency to keep the meaning game going. And we must not underestimate the seriousness with which Paulhan held up the example of cubism, however esoteric or futile the *papiers collés* may have seemed in 1945. His point is precisely that life's futilities are all we have to bear the burden of social understanding. Cubist space offers a new form for potentially universal agreement because it is founded on nothing: it has no reason to be. It is for 'all' people because it is entirely underdetermined – not imagined as being 'for' anything at all.

Next to nothing

The 'nothings' that precipitated Braque and Picasso's revolution in visuality and the Resistance fighter's decision to step into the unknown introduce a radical discontinuity into experience; they are free because they are unfounded. But if they are founded on nothing, they are not themselves 'nothing'. It is to articulate this distinction that I want to suggest they are 'next to nothing', belonging contingently to a regime of meaning, overlooked or dismissed, rather than reduced to absolutely nothing by the priorities of power. Thus, there are two modes of blindness in Paulhan's work: the blindness that is constitutive of human knowledge and language in that it *has* to exclude one face of the commonplace in order to constitute a regime of meaning; and the blindness, which is neither systematic nor total, to the remnants of a world. When this world, or order of things, ceases to hold together – in a time of war, for example, or extreme ideological strife such as during the late 1930s in France when language becomes an obstacle between people – these remnants offer the possibility of restoring an experience of community:

> There are times of inner misery when the sun and the forests, the houses and the streets suddenly lose their reason and their shine – they no longer speak to us. We become incapable of noble sentiment, or even of reasonable sentiment. That is when meaning attaches to absurd, silent things, scraps and leftovers in garbage cans ... We pursue through [these things] some secret sense. The pursuit makes our heads spin, takes us nowhere – and it would all seem pointless or idiotic if it were not that it is strangely accompanied by a sort of ecstasy. (Paulhan 1970c: 55)

Thus, the challenge that Paulhan envisages to political power does not so much seek to give voice to what is inaudible in society as it does to locate, even foster, those moments when the world falls silent and some form of recognition of what is left can occur. The temporality of recognition implies an initial forgetting or obliviousness to something, which will subsequently ring out with promise when it is all we have left to keep going. This recognition has no necessary political consequences, of course. It no more implies the perpetuation of a well-inscribed tradition than a radical shift in the forms of human experience. Thus, the archaic forms of proverbs can produce this experience of recognition and assent just as well as the revolutionary forms of the *papiers collés*. But nor is it a form of denegation. On the contrary, it encounters the world as incontrovertible, deep, mysterious, and open to us. Indeed, perhaps the most constant feature of Paulhan's work invoked to express the an experience of this voluminous community of being are the idiomatic or colloquial phrases, such as *'on n'a pas idée de ça'* which I quoted above. He uses these expressions to bridge the hiatus between words as clichés – fixed tokens of discourse – and words as truths, anchored in a particular expressive intention. But they also prompt an echo in the reader, an experience of their familiarity, as if one had voiced them oneself. More than just bivalent expressions or exemplars of the indeterminacy of the commonplace, they have a consistency that is known at the level of the body – the ear or the voice.

I have already located Paulhan's retraction – 'Let's say I said nothing' – at the end of *Les Fleurs de Tarbes* in the space of the hiatus between different regimes of meaning. I would like, in conclusion, to suggest that the attention in his writings on cubism to the unknowingness with which we have to fall into a new future, or out of an old pattern, enables us to read this retraction as a challenge to the reader, and not merely a suspension that delays both our own and his final word on the essay. It offers an opportunity to keep the process going precisely because it deprives us of the means. After all, it asks for our assent: 'let's say ...'. And what it wants us to assent to is nothing. But next to this nothing, hovering in the vicinity and catching our ear, is the almost casual familiarity of the expression, which means we might ignore it, if it were not for our desperate pursuit which here encounters a form that holds us enthralled.

References

Butler, J. 1997. *Excitable Speech: A Politics of the Performative*. London and New York: Routledge.

Paulhan, J. 1970a [1944]. 'Les Morts'. In *Œuvres complètes*, vol. 5. Paris: Le Cercle du livre précieux, 300–2.

Paulhan, J. 1970b [1944]. 'L'Abeille'. In *Œuvres complètes*, vol. 5. Paris: Le Cercle du livre précieux, 287–88.

Paulhan, J. 1970c [1953]. *La Peinture cubiste*. In *Œuvres complètes*, vol. 5. Paris: Le Cercle du livre précieux, 45–146.

Paulhan, J. 1987 [1952]. *Lettre aux Directeurs de la Résistance*. Paris: Editions Ramsay.

Paulhan, J. 1990. *Les Fleurs de Tarbes*. Edited by J.-C. Zylberstein. Paris: Gallimard.

Paulhan, J. 1992. *Choix de lettres*, vol II. Edited by D. Aury, J.-C. Zylberstein and B. Leuilliot. Paris: Gallimard.

Paulhan, J. 2004. *Correspondance Paulhan-Belaval*. Edited by A.-L. Milne. Paris: Gallimard.

Shapiro, G. 1999. *La Guerre des écrivains. 1940–1953*. Paris: Fayard.

Syrotinski, M. 1998. *Defying Gravity: Jean Paulhan's Interventions in Twentieth-Century French Intellectual History*. Albany, NY: State University of New York Press.

Verdès-Leroux, J. 1996. *Refus et violences: politique et littérature à l'extrême droite des années trente aux retombées de la Libération*. Paris: Gallimard.

Index

www.routledge.com/9780415528801

Related titles from Routledge

Donald Davidson
Life and Words

Edited by Maria Baghramian

Donald Davidson (1917-2004) was one of the most prominent philosophers of the second half of the twentieth century. His thinking about language, mind, and epistemology has shaped the views of several generations of philosophers. The present book brings together articles by a host of prominent contemporary philosophers to provide new interpretations of Davidson's key ideas about meaning, language and thought. The book opens with short commemorative pieces by contributors that give us glimpses of the life of a great philosopher, a beloved husband, colleague and teacher, and father. The article by Lepore and Ludwig and the ensuing heated debate with Fredrick Stoutland on how to interpret Davidson show why Davidson's legacy has become a disputed intellectual territory. The articles by Higginbotham, Pagin, Glüer, Smith and Child, all eminent philosophers of language, are prime examples of one strand in this legacy. The article by Gibbs gives us an opening to Davidson's enormous contribution to philosophy of mind. The book closes with a piece by Davidson, first published in 1995, where he brings together the various strands of his work in a Unified Theory of speech and action.

September 2012: 234 x 156: 272pp
Hb: 978-0-415-52880-1
£85 / $135

For more information and to order a copy visit
www.routledge.com/9780415528801

Available from all good bookshops

Related titles from Routledge

Disjunctivism

Edited by Marcus Willaschek

Does perception provide us with direct and unmediated access to the world around us? The so-called "argument from illusion" has traditionally been supposed to show otherwise: from the subject's point of view, perceptual illusions are often indistinguishable from veridical perceptions; hence, perceptual experience, as such, cannot provide us with knowledge of the world, but only with knowledge of how things appear to us. Disjunctive accounts of perceptual experience, first proposed by John McDowell and Paul Snowdon in the early 1980s and at the centre of current debates in the philosophy of perception, hotly debated today, have been proposed to block this argument. According to the traditional view, a case of perception and a subjectively indistinguishable illusion or hallucination can exemplify what is fundamentally the same kind of mental state even though they differ in how they relate to the non-mental environment. According to the disjunctive account, by contrast, the concept of perceptual experience should be seen as essentially disjunctive, encompassing (at least) two distinct kinds of mental states, namely genuinely world-involving perceptions and mere appearances.

This book was originally published as a special issue of *Philosophical Explorations: An International Journal for the Philosophy of Mind and Action.*

September 2012: 246 x 174: 184pp
Hb: 978-0-415-62306-3
£85 / $135

Available from all good bookshops

20879898R00072